An Analysis of

Michelle Alexander's

The New Jim Crow
Mass Incarceration in the Age of Colorblindness

Ryan Moore

Published by Macat International Ltd
24:13 Coda Centre, 189 Munster Road, London SW6 6AW.

Distributed exclusively by Routledge
2 Park Square, Milton Park, Abingdon, Oxon OX14 4RN
711 Third Avenue, New York, NY 10017, USA

Routledge is an imprint of the Taylor & Francis Group, an informa business

www.macat.com
info@macat.com

Cataloguing in Publication Data
A catalogue record for this book is available from the British Library.
Library of Congress Cataloguing-in-Publication Data is available upon request.
Cover illustration: Etienne Gilfillan

ISBN 978-1-912303-70-0 (hardback)
ISBN 978-1-912128-87-7 (paperback)
ISBN 978-1-912282-58-6 (e-book)

Notice
The information in this book is designed to orientate readers of the work under analysis,
to elucidate and contextualise its key ideas and themes, and to aid in the development
of critical thinking skills. It is not meant to be used, nor should it be used, as a
substitute for original thinking or in place of original writing or research. References and
notes are provided for informational purposes and their presence does not constitute
endorsement of the information or opinions therein. This book is presented solely for
educational purposes. It is sold on the understanding that the publisher is not engaged
to provide any scholarly advice. The publisher has made every effort to ensure that
this book is accurate and up-to-date, but makes no warranties or representations with
regard to the completeness or reliability of the information it contains. The information
and the opinions provided herein are not guaranteed or warranted to produce particular
results and may not be suitable for students of every ability. The publisher shall not be
liable for any loss, damage or disruption arising from any errors or omissions, or from
the use of this book, including, but not limited to, special, incidental, consequential or
other damages caused, or alleged to have been caused, directly or indirectly, by the
information contained within.

CONTENTS

THE MACAT LIBRARY

The Macat Library is a series of unique academic explorations of seminal works in the humanities and social sciences – books and papers that have had a significant and widely recognised impact on their disciplines. It has been created to serve as much more than just a summary of what lies between the covers of a great book. It illuminates and explores the influences on, ideas of, and impact of that book. Our goal is to offer a learning resource that encourages critical thinking and fosters a better, deeper understanding of important ideas.

Each publication is divided into three Sections: Influences, Ideas, and Impact. Each Section has four Modules. These explore every important facet of the work, and the responses to it.

This Section-Module structure makes a Macat Library book easy to use, but it has another important feature. Because each Macat book is written to the same format, it is possible (and encouraged!) to cross-reference multiple Macat books along the same lines of inquiry or research. This allows the reader to open up interesting interdisciplinary pathways.

To further aid your reading, lists of glossary terms and people mentioned are included at the end of this book (these are indicated by an asterisk [*] throughout) – as well as a list of works cited.

Macat has worked with the University of Cambridge to identify the elements of critical thinking and understand the ways in which six different skills combine to enable effective thinking.
Three allow us to fully understand a problem; three more give us the tools to solve it. Together, these six skills make up the **PACIER** model of critical thinking. They are:

ANALYSIS – understanding how an argument is built
EVALUATION – exploring the strengths and weaknesses of an argument
INTERPRETATION – understanding issues of meaning

CREATIVE THINKING – coming up with new ideas and fresh connections
PROBLEM-SOLVING – producing strong solutions
REASONING – creating strong arguments

To find out more, visit **WWW.MACAT.COM.**

CRITICAL THINKING AND *THE NEW JIM CROW*

Primary critical thinking skill: REASONING
Secondary critical thinking skill: CREATIVE THINKING

Michelle Alexander's *The New Jim Crow: Mass Incarceration in the Age of Colorblindness* is an unflinching dissection of the racial biases built into the American prison system. Named after the laws that enforced racial segregation in the southern United States until the mid-1960s, *The New Jim Crow* argues that while America is now legally a colorblind society – treating all races equally under the law – many factors combine to build profound racial weighting into the legal system.

The US now has the world's highest rate of incarceration, and a disproportionate percentage of the prison population is comprised of African-American men. Alexander's argument is that different legal factors have combined to mean both that African-Americans are more likely to be targeted by police, and to receive long jail sentences for their crimes. While many of Alexander's arguments and statistics are to be found in other books and authors' work, *The New Jim Crow* is a masterful example of the reasoning skills that communicate arguments persuasively. Alexander's skills are those fundamental to critical thinking reasoning: organizing evidence, examining other sides of the question, and synthesizing points to create an overall argument that is as watertight as it is persuasive.

ABOUT THE AUTHOR OF THE ORIGINAL WORK

Born in 1967, civil rights lawyer and law professor **Michelle Alexander**
first worked as a clerk for US Supreme Court Justice Harry A. Blackmun.
After taking a job as director of the American Civil Liberties Union's
Racial Justice Project in Northern California, she began investigating
institutional racism in America's criminal justice system. In 2010,
Alexander published *The New Jim Crow: Mass Incarceration in the Age of
Colorblindness*, highlighting how the US government's 'war on drugs' led to
the mass imprisonment of blacks. In 2011 her book won a National
Association for the Advancement of Colored People award for outstanding
nonfiction.

ABOUT THE AUTHOR OF THE ANALYSIS

Dr Ryan Moore holds PhDs in both sociology and cultural analysis from
the University of California, San Diego. He has taught at universities across
America and is the author of *Sells Like Teen Spirit: Music, Youth Culture, and
Social Crisis* (New York: NYU Press, 2009).

ABOUT MACAT

GREAT WORKS FOR CRITICAL THINKING

Macat is focused on making the ideas of the world's great thinkers
accessible and comprehensible to everybody, everywhere, in ways that
promote the development of enhanced critical thinking skills.

It works with leading academics from the world's top universities to
produce new analyses that focus on the ideas and the impact of the most
influential works ever written across a wide variety of academic disciplines.
Each of the works that sit at the heart of its growing library is an enduring
example of great thinking. But by setting them in context – and looking
at the influences that shaped their authors, as well as the responses they
provoked – Macat encourages readers to look at these classics and
game-changers with fresh eyes. Readers learn to think, engage and
challenge their ideas, rather than simply accepting them.

'Macat offers an amazing first-of-its-kind tool for interdisciplinary learning and research. Its focus on works that transformed their disciplines and its rigorous approach, drawing on the world's leading experts and educational institutions, opens up a world-class education to anyone.'

Andreas Schleicher
Director for Education and Skills, Organisation for Economic Co-operation and Development

'Macat is taking on some of the major challenges in university education ... They have drawn together a strong team of active academics who are producing teaching materials that are novel in the breadth of their approach.'

Prof Lord Broers,
former Vice-Chancellor of the University of Cambridge

'The Macat vision is exceptionally exciting. It focuses upon new modes of learning which analyse and explain seminal texts which have profoundly influenced world thinking and so social and economic development. It promotes the kind of critical thinking which is essential for any society and economy. This is the learning of the future.'

Rt Hon Charles Clarke, former UK Secretary of State for Education

'The Macat analyses provide immediate access to the critical conversation surrounding the books that have shaped their respective discipline, which will make them an invaluable resource to all of those, students and teachers, working in the field.'

Professor William Tronzo, University of California at San Diego

WAYS IN TO THE TEXT

KEY POINTS

- Michelle Alexander (b. 1967) is an American civil rights* lawyer and law professor.

- *The New Jim Crow: Mass Incarceration in the Age of Colorblindness* was first published in 2010; in it, Alexander argues that the mass incarceration* of people of color has created a racial caste system* akin to segregation.*

- *The New Jim Crow* reveals how a system of racial injustice and state control endures in a supposedly colorblind* society.

Who Is Michelle Alexander?

Michelle Alexander, the author of *The New Jim Crow: Mass Incarceration in the Age of Colorblindness* (2010), is a civil rights lawyer and an associate professor of law at Ohio State University in Columbus; "civil rights" here refers to those rights guaranteeing every citizen the equal enjoyment of political and social freedoms.

Alexander was born in Chicago on October 7, 1967; in 1975 her family moved to the San Francisco area, where her father worked as a salesman for the American technology corporation IBM.[1] A graduate of Vanderbilt University and Stanford Law School, after earning her law degree she served as clerk for Justice Harry A. Blackmun* on the Supreme Court of the United States—the nation's highest legal authority. Alexander later served as the director of the Racial Justice Project of the American Civil Liberties Union (ACLU)* in Northern California; the ACLU is an organization created to defend the individual liberties and rights guaranteed by the US Constitution. She won a Soros Justice Fellowship* in 2005 (funds supporting projects promoting reform and discussion of issues surrounding the US criminal justice system), which supported her as she wrote the book. During the same year, she accepted a joint appointment at the Kirwin Institute for the Study of Race and Ethnicity and the Moritz College of Law at Ohio State University.

Alexander says her experience at the ACLU directed her attention to institutional racism*—discrimination throughout the various structures and processes that define an institution—in the American criminal justice system. During her time there, she helped launch a national campaign against racial profiling,* a practice where police target people of a certain race, often African Americans, based on prejudicial stereotypes. This marked a shift from her previous focus on employment discrimination.

Since the publication of *The New Jim Crow,* Alexander has worked as a freelance writer, public speaker, and consultant for advocacy groups seeking to end mass incarceration—that is, imprisonment in in extremely high numbers. The book has emerged as a best-selling and influential text, making Alexander an important public figure; numerous national radio and television outlets have interviewed her. In 2011, *The New Jim Crow* won the Image Award for Outstanding Nonfiction from the National Association for the Advancement of Colored People (NAACP),* a long-established and influential civil rights body in the United States. Alexander's work has been acclaimed and endorsed by influential entrepreneurs, policymakers, political pundits, and media celebrities.

What Does *The New Jim Crow* Say?

Alexander focuses on how black men have suffered mass incarceration through the "war on drugs,"* a campaign started by the US government in the 1980s to crack down on illegal drug use and sales through increased policing and harsher sentencing of convicted abusers and dealers. She equates this to a new racial caste system—a system in which law or custom make upward mobility impossible for certain individuals.   Examples include apartheid* in twentieth-century South Africa, social hierarchies in India, and the Southern United States, where racial segregation via the so-called "Jim Crow"* laws passed in the 1880s and 1890s controlled and excluded African Americans until the 1960s. Comparing the war on drugs to the methods of segregation instituted following the Jim Crow laws, in *The New Jim Crow* Alexander describes a criminal justice system that exercises power over black people while claiming to be "colorblind."

Alexander places mass incarceration in a historical context of systemic racism in the United States. With the end of slavery, black people enjoyed what the social theorist and civil rights activist W. E. B. Du Bois* called a "brief moment in the sun" in the period following the American Civil War*[2] known as "Reconstruction,"* during which the federal government sought to protect the freedom of former slaves; the right to hold slaves played an important role in the Civil War, fought between 1861 and 1865 by the armies of the Northern and Southern ("Confederate") United States. The white Southern elite fought to halt and repeal these changes—eventually succeeding in creating a new system of segregation that disenfranchised black people and separated them from poor white people. This system—Jim Crow—remained in place until the American Civil Rights Movement* of the 1950s and 1960s pushed federal lawmakers to pass legislation to abolish it.   However, for Alexander, the mass incarceration of black people through the war on drugs replaced Jim Crow. Alexander argues that while the criminal justice system itself does not exercise direct discrimination in the post-civil rights era—because it is "colorblind"—the drug war controls and disempowers black people, especially black men.

Alexander describes colorblindness as a mentality that holds racism is a thing of the past because overt racism is taboo; most Americans do not hold racist views and the legal system no longer makes race a condition of civil rights. Put another way: colorblindness denies the persistence of racism in contemporary American society.

However, Alexander shows how institutional racism intervenes at every phase of the mass incarceration process, from policing, to legal deliberations, to life after prison. She shows how the war on drugs has given police extraordinary powers in stopping and searching anyone they view as suspicious. The federal government has also offered substantial financial incentives to police departments making mass arrests in the war on drugs. Black men are stopped and searched at highly disproportionate rates compared with white people, but these policing practices have withstood legal challenges except for cases where deliberate racial discrimination is proven. Facing the threat of harsh sentences for drug offenses, most defendants accept a plea bargain without ever going to trial. As a result, the war on drugs has been the leading factor behind the enormous increase in prison population in the United States.[3]

Why Does *The New Jim Crow* Matter?

The United States incarcerates more prisoners than any country in the world. In 30 years, the American penal population has increased from 300,000 to more than two million.[4] The war on drugs has been the most significant factor behind this upsurge in people going to prison. When the administration of US President Ronald Reagan* began this war in 1982, rates of drug use were actually on the decline.[5] However, the war on drugs disproportionately targets and punishes African Americans. Although people sell and use illegal drugs at roughly the same rates across racial groups, black men are 20 to 50 times more likely to be imprisoned on drug charges in some states.[6] The number of African Americans under correctional control—in prison or jail, probation or parole—is greater than the total number of slaves in 1850.[7]

Alexander argues that convicts continue to feel the effects of mass incarceration even after they are released from prison or jail. She compares the discrimination former criminals face to the denial of rights to Southern black people under segregation. While noting many differences between these racial caste systems, Alexander maintains that black people continue to encounter discrimination in a very similar fashion to Jim Crow. Under that Southern system, black people were systematically excluded and alienated in ways that appeared on the surface to be race-neutral. These included the poll tax* (a tax supposedly required from all people before they could vote) and the grandfather clause* (a law allowing white men to skip the poll tax). As a racial caste system, Jim Crow excluded and controlled black people by denying them political participation and economic opportunity. Alexander describes the difficulties drug offenders in contemporary America confront in getting jobs and finding places to live after they leave prison. Additionally, convicted criminals can lose their rights to vote and serve on juries—which Alexander compares to the denial of citizenship rights under Jim Crow.

Alexander's text exposes mass incarceration, and the legal system that supports it, as something that can strip people of fundamental rights of democratic citizenship such as the right to vote. She reveals it as a fundamentally racist framework designed to control people of color, especially black men. Though its tactics are colorblind in a legal sense, the war on drugs is rigged against black people—and Alexander insists that only a major social movement can abolish this racial caste system forever so that another system does not replace it. Alexander says Americans must engage in a meaningful dialog about race

that moves beyond the fiction of colorblindness.
NOTES

1   Arnie Cooper, "America's Drug War Has Led to a 'New and Improved' Racial
    Caste System, Argues Michelle Alexander," *Vanderbilt Magazine* (December
    2, 2013), accessed December 22, 2015, http://news.vanderbilt.edu/
    vanderbiltmagazine/strong-convictions/.

2   Michelle Alexander, *The New Jim Crow: Mass Incarceration in the Age of
    Colorblindness* (New York: New Press, 2010), 20.

3   Alexander, *The New Jim Crow*, 60.

4   Alexander, *The New Jim Crow*, 6.

5   Alexander, *The New Jim Crow*, 6.

6   Alexander, *The New Jim Crow*, 7.

7   Alexander, *The New Jim Crow*, 180.

SECTION 1
INFLUENCES

THE AUTHOR AND THE HISTORICAL CONTEXT

KEY POINTS

- *The New Jim Crow* challenges the systemic racism* of the war on drugs*—governmental policy designed to counter drug use in the United States—that has led to mass incarceration.*

- Michelle Alexander was a lawyer at the American Civil Liberties Union* (an organization created to defend the individual liberties and rights guaranteed by the US Constitution) when she began to see how mass incarceration functions as a racial caste system.*

- Alexander's critique sharpened as she refuted the notion of "colorblindness"* in the modern United States—the idea that the possibility of social and political equality had been secured for all under the law.

Why Read This Text?

In *The New Jim Crow: Mass Incarceration in the Age of Colorblindness* (2010), Michelle Alexander examines a crucial issue and source of injustice in American society: how the "war on drugs"—the effort by the US government to combat the trade and use of illegal narcotics—built a racial caste system comparable to forms of segregation* the nation had supposedly left behind.

She describes how the criminal justice system has made the United States the leading incarcerator in the world, with more than two million people in prison.[1] She also explains how the criminal justice system constrains people's lives after they leave prison, impacting their

> ❝ Ten years ago I would have argued strenuously against the central claim made here—namely, that something akin to a racial caste system currently exists in the United States ... Quite belatedly, I came to see that mass incarceration in the United States had, in fact, emerged as a stunningly comprehensive and well-disguised system of racialized social control that functions in a manner strikingly similar to Jim Crow. ❞
>
> Michelle Alexander, *The New Jim Crow: Mass Incarceration in the Age of Colorblindness*

ability to find work or housing. Alexander argues that the war on drugs is a selective war with an overall motivation of controlling black people, particularly young black men. This is why she compares it to the segregation of "Jim Crow":* discriminatory laws passed in the late nineteenth century that ensured the disenfranchisement of African Americans in the Southern United States. Originally, "Jim Crow" was the name of a popular song performed in minstrel shows in New York and other Northern cities before the American Civil War (a minstrel show is a form of entertainment in which white people perform caricatures of black people).[2] By the end of the nineteenth century, Jim Crow described a Southern social and political system that relegated black people to separate and inferior public spaces and institutions—while depriving them of civil and political rights.

The New Jim Crow has become a key text in the movement to end mass incarceration in the United States.[3] Alexander argues that abolishing the racial caste system upheld by the war on drugs must become a top priority for movements seeking racial justice. For this to happen, American society needs to move past the rhetoric of colorblindness into a frank conversation about race and racism.

Alexander insists that reforming the criminal justice system will not be enough—social justice movements must confront and eliminate the racial caste system. Otherwise, another form may replace it.

Author's Life

An acclaimed civil rights* lawyer and law professor, Michelle Alexander graduated from Vanderbilt University and Stanford Law School, and has held a joint appointment at the Kirwan Institute for the Study of Race and Ethnicity and the Moritz College of Law at Ohio State University since 2005: "Like many civil rights lawyers," she has explained, "I was inspired to attend law school by the civil rights victories of the 1950s and 1960s."[4]

Alexander says that as director of the Racial Justice Project of the American Civil Liberties Union (ACLU) in Northern California, she initially did not recognize the extent of racial injustice built into the criminal justice system. She saw it as an institution no more or less racist than any other. Though her task was to defend affirmative action* (the practice of offering special consideration in education and employment to racial minorities and women) and eliminate vestiges of segregation (particularly in education), Alexander began to shift her focus. "By the time I left the ACLU," she recalled, "I had come to suspect that I was wrong about the criminal justice system. It was not just another institution infected with racial bias but rather a different beast entirely."[5] She began to see mass incarceration as a racial caste system—one that contained many parallels to previous forms of segregation in America.

Author's Background

Alexander entered the legal profession in the 1990s, a generation after the Civil Rights Movement* of the 1950s and 1960s had secured racial equality under the law. Although conservatives were attacking these gains, the United States had become a more or less colorblind society. Alexander says that because she and her colleagues committed themselves to maintaining policies such as affirmative action, she initially failed to recognize the institutional racism behind the war on drugs—which met with little opposition when it first began and was not seen as an issue of racial injustice.

In *The New Jim Crow*, Alexander retraces the political factors that shaped the start of the war on drugs. While the administration of the US President Richard Nixon,* a Republican,* first declared war against drug use in 1971, another Republican president, Ronald Reagan,* in office between 1981 and 1989, fully mobilized the federal government into a "get tough" approach to drug use and sales.[6] Beginning in 1982, Reagan's war on drugs was launched on multiple fronts:

- Greater discretion for police in stops and searches
- Grants for local police to purchase military equipment
- Longer sentences for drug offenders
- Making drug offenders ineligible for public housing and other government benefits.

During the Nixon administration, the Republican Party had built an electoral coalition that depended on support from working-class white people, especially in the South. Republicans built this coalition by appealing to cultural conservatism in a backlash against the social changes of the 1960s. While no longer able to directly invoke race in the post-civil rights era (that is, the years following the mid-1960s), Republicans tapped into racial hostility and fear through the seemingly colorblind rhetoric of crime, drugs, welfare, and states' rights.

Soon the Democratic Party also adopted this language about the need to get "tough on crime" and show "zero tolerance" for drug offenders. President Bill Clinton* signed a $30 billion crime bill in 1994 as Democrats tried to compete with the Republicans for the lead role in tackling the issues of drugs, crime, and welfare reform.

Supported by a bipartisan consensus, the war on drugs became permanent—and as it escalated, incarceration rates continued to increase as well.

NOTES

1. Michelle Alexander, *The New Jim Crow: Mass Incarceration in the Age of Colorblindness* (New York: New Press, 2010), 6.

2. Eric Lott, *Love and Theft: Blackface and the American Minstrelsy* (New York: Oxford University Press, 1993).

3. Cornel West, foreword to *The New Jim Crow: Mass Incarceration in the Age of Colorblindness*, by Michelle Alexander (New York: New Press, 2010), IX–XI.

4. Alexander, *The New Jim Crow*, 3.

5. Alexander, *The New Jim Crow*, 4.

6. Alexander, *The New Jim Crow*, 5.

MODULE 2
ACADEMIC CONTEXT

KEY POINTS

- *The New Jim Crow* is mainly concerned with institutional or "structural" racism* in the criminal justice system.

- Legal scholars, criminologists* (scholars of criminal behavior and criminal law), sociologists* (scholars of social structures and social behavior), and activist intellectuals have undertaken previous studies of mass incarceration.*

- Alexander was especially influenced by the critical analyses of mass incarceration conducted by other scholars in the legal profession.

The Work in its Context

Michelle Alexander's *The New Jim Crow: Mass Incarceration in the Age of Colorblindness* speaks to two fields of study concerned with racial inequalities. The first field concerns the broad analysis of institutional or "structural" racism, which suggests that racial inequalities are more than just racist attitudes held by people, particularly in the era following the struggle for civil rights* for minorities in the United States. In an officially colorblind* society—where a clear majority of Americans say they are not prejudiced and explicit racism is taboo—these scholars examine how racial inequalities continue to reproduce themselves in a systemic manner. The second field includes those more narrowly concerned with the criminal justice system. The government's ongoing "war on drugs" and the enormous increase of the American prison population it has brought have led scholars and advocates to examine the connections between institutional racism and mass incarceration.

> ❝ The unfortunate reality we must face is that racism manifests itself not only in individual attitudes, but also in the basic structure of society. Academics have developed complicated theories and obscure jargon in an effort to describe what is now referred to as structural racism, yet the concept is fairly straightforward. ❞
>
> Michelle Alexander, *The New Jim Crow: Mass Incarceration in the Age of Colorblindness*

The New Jim Crow advances both fields of scholarship and social criticism. Michelle Alexander broadened the analysis of institutional racism by comparing mass incarceration to the segregation* instituted in the Southern United States in the late nineteenth century by the Jim Crow* laws repealed in the mid-1960s—and situating it as the latest in a long line of racial caste systems.* She also expanded the definition of mass incarceration by examining how offenders face continued discrimination and exclusion from mainstream society after their release from prison. This allowed her to extend her comparisons with the Jim Crow period and reveal historical parallels between two racial caste systems that perpetuate legalized discrimination and political disenfranchisement.[1]

Overview of the Field

Alexander addressed many ongoing concerns about the connections between institutional racism and the war on drugs. Among other legal scholars, the criminal law scholar Michael H. Tonry* has undertaken the most comprehensive studies of mass incarceration in relation to racism. Since the 1990s, his work has examined the connections between race, crime, and punishment.[2] Marc Mauer,* Executive Director of The Sentencing Project* (a nonprofit sentencing reform group), also conducted groundbreaking investigations into the links between race, class, and the criminal justice system.[3] Alexander's analysis builds on these earlier studies—which, though the first to reveal the systemic racial biases of the drug war, reached much smaller audiences than *The New Jim Crow*.

Additionally, the subfield of critical criminology—the study of crime from the perspective of Marxism* and conflict theories of society—also produced important studies of mass incarceration (according to Marxist analysis, class conflict, very roughly, is the principal driver of social discord generally). The criminologist Todd R. Clear* examined how the growth of America's penal population has adverse effects on inner-city neighborhoods—and how mass incarceration worsens the social problems it claims to solve.[4] The French sociologist Loïc Wacquant* explored the economic basis of prisons: neoliberal* capitalism,* according to which markets are allowed to function without government hindrance, creates a surplus population of poor youth; mass incarceration is the booming industry that absorbs and controls them.[5]

Finally, some critical analyses of mass incarceration originated with activist intellectuals who scrutinized and criticized the economic and political links between institutional racism and increasing imprisonment.[6] The radical scholar Angela Y. Davis* has investigated what she calls the "prison-industrial complex.*"[7] The social historian Mike Davis* invented this term in 1995 as he condemned the overlapping economic and political interests behind California's booming penal system.[8]

Academic Influences

Alexander engages both wide-ranging theories of structural racism and empirical studies of race, crime, and mass incarceration. To explain how racial inequalities can persist in a colorblind society, she refers to a famous "birdcage" metaphor invoked by the political theorist Iris Marion Young.*[9] Alexander described how Young used this metaphor to illustrate how structural racism can go unnoticed: "If one thinks about racism by examining only one wire of the cage, or one form of disadvantage, it is difficult to understand how and why the bird is trapped."[10]

Other legal scholars who had earlier written about mass incarceration clearly influenced Alexander as well. After publishing *The New Jim Crow*, she wrote the foreword to an illustrated version of Marc Mauer's *Race to Incarcerate* and recalled that "there was one book— and only one book—that I viewed as utterly indispensable to my work: *Race to Incarcerate*."[11] She also cites and quotes from the work of Wacquant and Clear. In describing how mass incarceration disrupts and destroys black families and inner-city neighborhoods, Alexander writes that Clear "powerfully demonstrates that imprisonment has reached such extreme levels in many urban communities that a prison sentence and/or a felon label poses a greater threat to urban families than crime itself."[12]

One prominent figure missing from *The New Jim Crow*, however, is Angela Y. Davis. Alexander does not refer to Davis or the concept of the prison-industrial complex at any point. This shows the difference between Davis's argument (which focuses more on the economic and political interests involved in private prisons) and Alexander's—which compares the current system with older caste systems more motivated by racial exclusion.

To be sure, *The New Jim Crow* covered some familiar terrain—a fact Alexander acknowledges—but her concept of a modern racial caste system in a supposedly colorblind America also broke new ground.

NOTES

1   Michelle Alexander, *The New Jim Crow: Mass Incarceration in the Age of Colorblindness* (New York: New Press, 2010), 191–3.

2   Michael H. Tonry, *Malign Neglect: Race, Crime, and Punishment in America*

(New York: Oxford University Press, 1995).

3   Marc Mauer, *Race to Incarcerate* (New York: New Press, 1999).

4   Todd R. Clear, *Imprisoning Communities: How Mass Incarceration Makes Disadvantaged Neighborhoods Worse* (New York: NYU Press, 2009).

5   Loïc Wacquant, *Prisons of Poverty* (Minneapolis, MN: University of Minnesota Press, 2009).

6   Christian Parenti, *Lockdown America: Police and Prison in the Age of Crisis* (New York: Verso, 1999).

7   Angela Y. Davis, *Are Prisons Obsolete?* (New York: Seven Stories Press, 2003).

8   Mike Davis, "Hell Factories in the Field: A Prison-Industrial Complex," *The Nation* (February 20, 1995).

9   Iris Marion Young, *Inclusion and Democracy* (New York: Oxford University Press, 2000), 92–9.

10 Alexander, *The New Jim Crow*, 184.

11 Michelle Alexander, foreword to *Race to Incarcerate: A Graphic Retelling*, by Marc Mauer and Sabrina Jones (New York: New Press, 2013), VII.

12 Alexander, *The New Jim Crow*, 237.

MODULE 3
THE PROBLEM

KEY POINTS

- *The New Jim Crow* followed several other scholarly works that investigated the links between institutional racism* and mass incarceration* in the United States.

- Beginning in the late 1990s, critics of mass incarceration made various arguments about the presence of a prison-industrial complex*—a structure exploiting society through mass incarceration for private profit.

- While Alexander is not explicit about her position, she avoids the term "prison-industrial complex" and the concerns surrounding it. This distinguishes her argument from those that highlight the economic factors driving mass incarceration.

Core Question

Michelle Alexander addressed how the criminal justice system, despite its claim to colorblindness,* perpetuates racial inequality and injustice. *The New Jim Crow: Mass Incarceration in the Age of Colorblindness* followed studies by legal scholars, criminologists,* sociologists,* and activist intellectuals that investigated the links between institutional racism and mass incarceration. During the administration of President Ronald Reagan* (1981–9), there was a broad consensus in American society and little dissent from racial justice advocates about the "war on drugs." However, as the penal population multiplied, and racial disparities in incarceration rates emerged, some scholars and activists began to scrutinize the drug war and the criminal justice system.

Alexander took the unique step of calling mass incarceration a racial "caste system."* She wrote, "The system operates through our

> ❝ What is completely missed in the rare public debates today about the plight of African Americans is that a huge percentage of them are not free to move up at all. It is not just that they lack opportunity, attend poor schools, or are plagued by poverty. They are barred by law from doing so. And the major institutions with which they come into contact are designed to prevent their mobility. To put the matter starkly: The current system of control permanently locks a huge percentage of the African American community out of the mainstream society and economy. ❞
>
> Michelle Alexander, *The New Jim Crow: Mass Incarceration in the Age of Colorblindness*

criminal justice institutions, but it functions more like a caste system than a system of crime control. Viewed from this perspective, the so-called underclass is better understood as an undercaste—a lower caste of individuals who are permanently barred by law and custom from mainstream society."[1] How, she asked, could these inequalities and injustices persist in a legal system that had officially abolished racial distinctions?

"Although this new system of racialized social control purports to be colorblind, it creates and maintains racial hierarchy much as earlier systems of control did. Like Jim Crow* (and slavery), mass incarceration operates as a tightly networked system of laws, policies, customs and institutions that operate collectively to ensure the subordinate status of a group defined largely by race."[2]

The Participants

During the 1990s, two criminal law professors, Michael H. Tonry* and Elliot Currie,* and the social worker Jerome G. Miller* presented some of the first analyses of institutional racism in the war on drugs and the criminal justice system.[3] However, the Harvard law professor Randall Kennedy* challenged their reasoning in his 1997 book *Race, Crime, and the Law*. For him, racial justice in the American legal system was vastly improved and would continue to progress. He rejected claims of racial bias in the drug war and emphasized the support for tougher policing and sentencing within the black community.[4]

Writers and academics who disagreed with Kennedy saw it as more of a matter of politics and profit. The radical social theorist Angela Y. Davis* began talking about the "prison-industrial complex" in her lectures and writings in 1997–8;[5] the social historian Mike Davis* had previously used the term to describe California's penal system, and the investigative journalist Eric Schlosser* also applied it to his 1998 article in *The Atlantic* magazine on the intersections of economics and politics in the prison system.[6] Some critics of mass incarceration rejected the concept, however; the French sociologist Loïc Wacquant,* for example, argued that it overstates the significance of private economic interests and the extent of institutional unity at work in mass incarceration.[7]

The Contemporary Debate

While a number of scholars and activists had highlighted how the war on drugs created racial inequalities in the criminal justice system by the end of the 1990s, police crackdowns, longer sentencing, and various "get tough" policies continued to enjoy wide popular support and a bipartisan political consensus. Indeed, the administration of Bill Clinton* (1993–2001), politically dissimilar to that of Ronald Reagan, enacted some of the most draconian measures. A civil rights* lawyer at the time, Alexander recalled that the systemic racism of mass incarceration initially eluded her: "Never did I seriously consider the possibility that a new racial caste system was operating in this country. The new system had been developed and implemented swiftly, and it was largely invisible, even to people, like me, who spent most of their waking hours fighting for justice."[8]

Alexander does not invoke the prison-industrial complex identified by activists and critics in the late 1990s. *The New Jim Crow* only briefly discusses for-profit prisons, the economics of the penal system, or the use of prison labor. *The New Jim Crow* also contains no references to Angela Y. Davis, the most prominent critic of the prison-industrial complex.

On the other hand, Alexander often quotes from the work of Loïc Wacquant, who dismisses the notion of a prison-industrial complex and the economic significance of mass incarceration. Summing up Wacquant's thesis, she writes, "The new system does not seek primarily to benefit unfairly from black labor, as earlier caste systems have, but instead views African Americans as largely irrelevant and unnecessary to the newly structured economy—an economy that is no longer driven by unskilled labor."[9]

Alexander's argument highlights a disturbing facet of American society: black people who were slaves in one caste system became prisoners in another.

NOTES

1   Michelle Alexander, *The New Jim Crow: Mass Incarceration in the Age of Colorblindness* (New York: New Press, 2010), 13.

2   Alexander, *The New Jim Crow*, 13.

3   Michael H. Tonry, *Malign Neglect: Race, Crime, and Punishment in America* (New York: Oxford University Press, 1995); Jerome G. Miller, *Search and Destroy: African-American Males in the Criminal Justice System* (New York: Cambridge University Press, 1996); Elliot Currie, *Crime and Punishment in America* (New York: Metropolitan Books, 1998).

4   Randall Kennedy, *Race, Crime, and the Law* (New York: Pantheon Books, 1997).

5   Angela Y. Davis, "Masked Racism: Reflections on the Prison Industrial Complex," Colorlines (September 10, 1998), accessed November 14, 2015, http://www.colorlines.com/articles/masked-racism-reflections-prison-industrial-complex.

6   Mike Davis, "Hell Factories in the Field: A Prison-Industrial Complex," *The Nation* (February 20, 1995); Eric Schlosser, "The Prison-Industrial Complex," *The Atlantic* (December 1998).

7   Prison Culture: How the PIC Structures Our World ..., accessed November 14, 2015, http://www.usprisonculture.com/blog/2010/09/15/speaking-for-himself-professor-loic-wacquant-corrects-my-characterization-of-his-critique-of-the-concept-of-the-prison-industrial-complex/.

8   Alexander, *The New Jim Crow*, 3.

9   Alexander, *The New Jim Crow*, 219.

MODULE 4
THE AUTHOR'S CONTRIBUTION

KEY POINTS

- Michelle Alexander concluded that mass incarceration* has created a racial caste system* similar to the segregation* of Jim Crow* (shorthand for the disenfranchising laws and customs enforced against black people in the Southern United States following slavery).

- While other scholars had investigated the link between racism and the war on drugs,* Alexander made a distinct contribution by comparing it to Jim Crow.

- *The New Jim Crow* departed from Alexander's previous advocacy work; in it, she argued that racial justice organizations also needed to shift their focus to mass incarceration.

Author's Aims

By the time Michelle Alexander wrote *The New Jim Crow: Mass Incarceration in the Age of Colorblindness*, numerous scholars, journalists, and activists had revealed the racial biases of the US government's so-called "war on drugs" and the criminal justice system. Her unique contribution illuminates the parallels between mass incarceration and prior forms of segregation.

Alexander begins to accomplish this aim by demonstrating how both systems arose in comparable times of political crisis. The first chapter of *The New Jim Crow* sketches the history of America's racial caste systems: from slavery to segregation to mass incarceration. Comparing the origins of Jim Crow and the war on drugs, Alexander found that both systems began with "a desire among white elites to

> ❝ There are important differences between mass
> incarceration and Jim Crow, to be sure ... but when
> we step back and view the system as a whole, there is
> a profound sense of déjà vu. There is a familiar stigma
> and shame. There is an elaborate system of control,
> complete with political disenfranchisement and legalized
> discrimination in every major realm of economic and
> social life. And there is the production of racial meaning
> and racial boundaries. ❞
>
> Michelle Alexander, *The New Jim Crow: Mass Incarceration in the Age of
> Colorblindness*

exploit the resentments, vulnerabilities and racial biases of poor and
working-class white people for political and economic gain."[1] These
alliances of elites and the lower classes, supported by a common
identity of whiteness, secured political consent for systems devised to
control black people.

Alexander turns her comparative approach from history to the law
in the following chapters of *The New Jim Crow*, revealing further
parallels between Jim Crow and mass incarceration by showing how
they both utilize legal discrimination and political disenfranchisement.
Alexander examines legal history to show how the Supreme Court
(the nation's highest legal authority) has played a crucial role in
upholding each racial caste system. With regard to mass incarceration,
Alexander argues that "the Court has closed the courthouse doors to
claims of racial bias at every stage of the criminal justice process, from
stops and searches to plea bargaining and sentencing."[2] Just as the
Supreme Court immunized Jim Crow from legal challenge, it now
protects the mass incarceration of black people by rejecting charges of
systemic racism.*

Approach

The New Jim Crow is distinguished by Alexander's legal expertise and her historical comparisons. The legal and historical parallels between Jim Crow and mass incarceration through the war on drugs lead Alexander to define them as related forms of an enduring racial caste system. The term "racial caste system" marks another unique feature of *The New Jim Crow*; Alexander says she uses it "to denote a stigmatized racial group locked into an inferior position by law and custom."[3]

As she examines legal precedents set out by the Supreme Court, Alexander crafts a distinctive argument about how official colorblindness* actually preserves racial inequality. She discusses in detail the 1987 verdict in the case known as "McCleskey v. Kemp,"* an unsuccessful challenge to racial bias in the death penalty. In "closing the courthouse doors" to claims of systemic racism, the verdict created an impact Alexander compares to previous landmark cases that protected segregation and slavery ("McCleskey v. Kemp and its progeny serve much the same function as Dred Scott and Plessy").[4]

Alexander's analysis of Jim Crow's legal foundations, and how they repeated themselves in mass incarceration, shapes her historical perspective on the cyclical patterns of racial caste systems: "Since the nation's founding, African Americans repeatedly have been controlled through institutions such as slavery and Jim Crow, which appear to die, but then are reborn in new form, tailored to the needs and constraints of the time."[5] She also finds parallels between political reaction against Reconstruction* (the occupation of the Southern states by Northern troops after the American Civil War* of 1861–5) and the Civil Rights Movement*—flash points that ignited white racism motivated the development of these racial caste systems. Alexander concludes: "It is during this period of uncertainty that the backlash intensifies and a new form of racialized social control begins to take hold."[6]

Following Reconstruction, the white Southern elite fought these changes by instituting a new system of segregation that disenfranchised black people and separated them from poor white people. This system known as Jim Crow remained in place until the Civil Rights Movement of the 1950s and 1960s pushed the federal government to pass legislation that abolished it.

Contribution in Context

For at least a dozen years before Alexander published *The New Jim Crow* in 2010, many other scholars and activists had crafted arguments about the institutional racism of the war on drugs, the criminal justice system, and mass incarceration but Alexander made a unique contribution by comparing this phenomenon to Jim Crow. Along with the academic theorists who probed structural racism, Alexander demonstrates how this racial caste system can thrive in a colorblind society. The African American activist and philosophy professor Cornel West* sums up Alexander's contribution by writing, "[Her] nuanced historical narrative tracing the unconscionable treatment and brutal control of black people—slavery, Jim Crow, mass incarceration—takes us beneath the political surfaces and lays bare the structures of a racial caste system alive and well in the age of colorblindness."[7]

Since the late 1990s, numerous books and articles have argued against the system of the war on drugs, the growing prison population, and what the radical social theorist Angela Y. Davis calls the "prison-industrial complex." *The New Jim Crow* has outsold these other works though and profoundly influenced a new generation of racial justice activists.[8] West called it "the secular bible for a new social movement in early twenty-first century America."[9] Alexander offers provocative arguments about how racial justice advocates need to direct their attention and efforts toward the mass incarceration issue. "One day," she writes, "civil rights* organizations may be embarrassed by how long it took them to move out of denial and do the hard work necessary to end mass incarceration."[10]

NOTES

1   Michelle Alexander, *The New Jim Crow: Mass Incarceration in the Age of Colorblindness* (New York: New Press, 2010), 191.

2   Alexander, *The New Jim Crow*, 194.

3   Alexander, *The New Jim Crow*, 12.

4   Alexander, *The New Jim Crow*, 194.

5   Alexander, *The New Jim Crow*, 21.

6   Alexander, *The New Jim Crow*, 21–2.

7   Cornel West, foreword to *The New Jim Crow: Mass Incarceration in the Age of Colorblindness*, by Michelle Alexander (New York: New Press, 2010), x.

8   Jennifer Schuessler, "Drug Policy as Race Policy: Best Seller Galvanizes the Debate," *New York Times* (March 6, 2012).

9   West, foreword, ix.

10 Alexander, *The New Jim Crow*, 224.

SECTION 2
IDEAS

MODULE 5
MAIN IDEAS

KEY POINTS

- The key theme of *The New Jim Crow* centers on systemic racism* in the criminal justice system, masked by an official colorblindness* under the law.

- Michelle Alexander contends that mass incarceration* from the US government's "war on drugs"* has created a racial caste system* that replaced segregation.*

- Alexander frames her argument in an accessible style intended to reach activists, policymakers, and the general public.

Key Themes

In *The New Jim Crow: Mass Incarceration in the Age of Colorblindness*, Michelle Alexander argues that the war on drugs created a racial caste system. Alexander maintains that the war on drugs—though stemming from an officially colorblind criminal justice system—is structured to contain and exclude people of color. She situates mass incarceration in a historical context, comparing it to the previous racial caste systems of slavery and segregation. Alexander concludes that mass incarceration fueled by the war on drugs shares many similarities with Jim Crow* segregation.

Alexander develops four key themes in *The New Jim Crow*:

- Mass incarceration is a racial caste system, not a colorblind response to crime.
- The war on drugs selectively targets black and brown people for offenses that typically go unpunished among white people.
- Mass incarceration is a reaction to the end of Jim Crow

> **❝** This book argues that mass incarceration is, metaphorically, the New Jim Crow and that all those who care about social justice should fully commit themselves to dismantling the new racial caste system. Mass incarceration—not attacks on affirmative action or lax civil rights enforcement—is the most damaging manifestation of the backlash against the Civil Rights Movement. **❞**
>
> Michelle Alexander, *The New Jim Crow: Mass Incarceration in the Age of Colorblindness*

     segregation attained by the Civil Rights Movement.*
- The US Supreme Court has consistently defended the criminal justice system against legal challenges to institutional racism.

"Following the collapse of each system of control," Alexander writes, "there has been a period of confusion—transition—in which those who are most committed to racial hierarchy search for new means to achieve their goals within rules of the game as currently defined."[1] Thus in the post-civil rights* era, when it is no longer acceptable for politicians to speak in overtly racist terms, racial prejudice adopts the coded language of fights against crime, drugs, and welfare.

Exploring the Ideas

The New Jim Crow describes how stages of mass incarceration work against people of color, despite being formally colorblind. The war on drugs gave police the power to stop and search *anyone* under *any* pretext. Although these practices violate the US Constitution's Fourth Amendment protections against unreasonable search and seizure, courts uphold them if police can attain even the flimsiest form of consent. The federal government has also encouraged local police departments to prioritize the drug war with rewards of cash grants and military hardware. According to Alexander, "it is doubtful that the drug war would have been launched with such intensity on the ground but for the bribes offered for law enforcement's cooperation."[2]

Police have primarily focused on inner-city ghettos in fighting the war on drugs, despite the fact that white people and black people use and sell drugs at similar rates. As a predictable result, people of color comprise a disproportionate number of arrests for drug offenses— three-quarters of those imprisoned for drugs have been black or Latino.[3] Additionally, systemic discrimination continues in the sentencing phase. One crucial feature of the war on drugs involves much more stringent mandatory minimum sentencing* for possession of crack—a potent form of crystallized cocaine that is smoked—than powder cocaine. Whereas mandatory minimum sentences of five years are imposed for anyone caught with 500 grams of powder cocaine, the same sentence has applied to those with just five grams of crack.[4] The vast majority of people arrested for crack possession are black, while cocaine offenders are predominantly white.[5]

Language and Expression

Alexander seems to have written *The New Jim Crow* for activists, policymakers, and the general public: it is not a strictly an academic work. As she states, "What this book is intended to do—the only thing it is intended to do—is to stimulate a much-needed conversation about the role of the criminal justice system in creating and perpetuating racial hierarchy in the United States."[6] In keeping with this purpose, her prose is concise, direct, and easy to grasp.

She devotes a large portion of *The New Jim Crow* to a discussion of Supreme Court cases that have sustained the war on drugs. Drawing on her expertise as a civil rights lawyer, Alexander examines decisions that have made it impossible to challenge the racial bias of the drug war without evidence of conscious, intentional discrimination. One Supreme Court case she discusses at length is McCleskey v. Kemp,* a 1986–7 case that challenged the death penalty on the grounds that defendants were more than four times likelier to receive a death sentence if the victim was white and the perpetrator black.[7] In a 5–4 decision, the Court ruled that the death penalty did not constitute unequal treatment under law unless defense attorneys could prove the prosecution or the jury acted in a deliberately racist manner. McCleskey v. Kemp established a precedent for subsequent challenges to the criminal justice system, such as the disparity in sentencing for crack and cocaine. Alexander concluded: "There is good reason to believe that, despite appearances, the McCleskey decision was not really about the death penalty at all; rather, the Court's opinion was driven by a desire to immunize the entire criminal justice system from claims of racial bias."[8]

NOTES

1   Michelle Alexander, *The New Jim Crow: Mass Incarceration in the Age of Colorblindness* (New York: New Press, 2010), 21.

2   Alexander, *The New Jim Crow*, 83.

3   Alexander, *The New Jim Crow*, 98.

4   In 2010, President Obama signed the Fair Sentencing Act, which increased the threshold of mandatory minimum sentencing for crack to 28 grams.

5   Alexander, *The New Jim Crow*, 112.

6   Alexander, *The New Jim Crow*, 16.

7   Alexander, *The New Jim Crow*, 110.

8   Alexander, *The New Jim Crow*, 111.

SECONDARY IDEAS

KEY POINTS

- Michelle Alexander supports her argument by revealing how drug offenders continue to encounter discrimination after their release from prison.

- Investigating post-prison life, Alexander shows how mass incarceration* becomes a lifelong process akin to Jim Crow* segregation.*

- Alexander shows how ex-offenders face tremendous obstacles in securing employment, housing, and public assistance.

Other Ideas

Michelle Alexander's *The New Jim Crow: Mass Incarceration in the Age of Colorblindness* is primarily concerned with mass incarceration resulting from the "war on drugs." However, she argues, mass incarceration does not end when people leave prison; for her, it includes "the larger web of laws, rules, policies, and customs that control those labeled criminals both in and out of prison."[1] While more than two million people sit behind bars, approximately five million more are on probation or parole—in total, one in every 31 adults is caught in the system of mass incarceration.[2]

Alexander's analysis of life after prison extends her theme that mass incarceration compares to Jim Crow. She demonstrates how legal forms of discrimination and exclusion continue to afflict ex-convicts long after they have paid their debt to society. While Alexander's main focus involves factors leading to imprisonment, she deepens her analysis by discussing how the stigma of incarceration impedes black

> ❝ In many respects, release from prison does not represent the beginning of freedom but instead a cruel new phase of stigmatization and control. Myriad laws, rules, and regulations discriminate against ex-offenders and effectively prevent their meaningful re-integration into the mainstream economy and society. I argue that the shame and stigma of the 'prison label' is, in many respects, more damaging to the African American community than the shame and stigma associated with Jim Crow. ❞
>
> Michelle Alexander, *The New Jim Crow: Mass Incarceration in the Age of Colorblindness*

people on many crucial levels: the ability to get work, find housing, and reintegrate into mainstream society. The similarities with Jim Crow persist outside of prison: "A criminal record today authorizes precisely the forms of discrimination we supposedly left behind— discrimination in employment, housing, education, public benefits and jury service."[3]

Beyond these formal mechanisms of discrimination and exclusion, a general stigma and loss of respect within one's community also ensues. In sum, "Today a criminal freed from prison has scarcely more rights, and arguably less respect, than a freed slave or a black person living 'free' in Mississippi at the height of Jim Crow."[4]

Exploring the Ideas

Alexander describes the various ways people are discriminated against and excluded from mainstream society after they leave prison. For the more than 650,000 people released from prison each year, finding a place to live is the most immediate concern—and often the most difficult task.[5] One study revealed that a quarter of the residents in homeless shelters had been incarcerated within the last year.[6] At the behest of then-President Bill Clinton,* in 1996, the US Department of Housing and Urban Development (HUD)* adopted a "One Strike, You're Out" policy that automatically excluded drug offenders from eligibility for public housing.[7]

Finding work represents another major difficulty for newly released offenders. In the retail and service sectors—where most new jobs are now created—the reluctance to hire people with criminal records is greatest. Alexander cites numerous examples of job advertisements that explicitly exclude people with criminal histories, concluding: "Millions find themselves locked out of the legal economy, and no one with a record has a more difficult time getting hired than black men."[8]

Yet the obstacles people who get out of prison face do not end with housing and employment. Alexander describes how former offenders are burdened with sizeable financial debts to probation departments, courts, and child-support enforcement offices.[9] The welfare-reform legislation signed by President Clinton in 1996 also made people with drug-related felony convictions ineligible for public assistance.[10] The vast majority of states deny people the right to vote while on parole, and some continue to deny them voting rights for years after that.[11]

Overlooked

Reviews of *The New Jim Crow* have largely focused on Alexander's analysis of systemic racism as it relates to mass incarceration but have paid less attention to her prescriptions for resisting and changing this racial caste system.* As Alexander contends, the first step is for racial justice advocates to move beyond the ideology of colorblindness* informing previous generations that followed the Civil Rights Movement.* "It is not an overstatement," she argues, "to say the systematic mass incarceration of people of color in the United States would not have been possible in the post-civil rights* era if the nation had not fallen under the spell of a callous colorblindness."[12]

Perhaps more controversially, Alexander suggests that it may be time to give up the "racial bribe" of affirmative action,* which grants preferred status to racial minorities and women in areas from college admissions to employment. She questions whether affirmative action has actually disguised the new racial caste system—reinforcing the myth that anyone can make it in America while fostering a "trickle down theory of racial justice"[13] She maintains that exceptional instances of success among African Americans support the ideology that race no longer matters in the United States. Therefore, if race no longer matters, it is easier to condemn the incarcerated for freely choosing their fate. "So long as some readily identifiable African Americans are doing well," Alexander states, "the system is largely immunized from racial critique."[14]

Moreover, in an ironic twist, affirmative action has obscured institutional racism* further due to the greater inclusion of black people in America's police departments. As Alexander notes, "The existence of black police chiefs and black officers would be no more encouraging today than the presence of black slave drivers and black plantation owners hundreds of years ago."[15]

NOTES

1   Michelle Alexander, *The New Jim Crow: Mass Incarceration in the Age of Colorblindness* (New York: New Press, 2010), 13.

2   Alexander, *The New Jim Crow*, 60.

3   Alexander, *The New Jim Crow*, 141.

4   Alexander, *The New Jim Crow*, 141.

5   Alexander, *The New Jim Crow*, 148.

6   Alexander, *The New Jim Crow*, 147.

7   Alexander, *The New Jim Crow*, 145–6.

8   Alexander, *The New Jim Crow*, 154.

9   Alexander, *The New Jim Crow*, 154–5.

10 Alexander, *The New Jim Crow*, 157.

11 Alexander, *The New Jim Crow*, 158.

12 Alexander, *The New Jim Crow*, 240–1.

13 Alexander, *The New Jim Crow*, 245.

14 Alexander, *The New Jim Crow*, 248.

15 Alexander, *The New Jim Crow*, 250.

ACHIEVEMENT

KEY POINTS

- *The New Jim Crow* has made a major impact through its provocative argument that mass incarceration* creates a racial caste system* akin to segregation.*

- Michelle Alexander published *The New Jim Crow* shortly after Barack Obama's* election as US president in 2009. She demonstrated the persistence of systemic racism,* even in a country that had just elected its first black president.

- Though Alexander presented a strong argument about the similarities between mass incarceration and Jim Crow,* she recognized limits to the analogy.

Assessing the Argument

By assembling an abundance of statistical and legal evidence, in *The New Jim Crow: Mass Incarceration in the Age of Colorblindness* Michelle Alexander successfully revealed the parallels between mass incarceration and Jim Crow. Her book was a "surprise best seller" and has proven to be influential among activists and even some policymakers.[1] Several other books had previously argued that mass incarceration resulting from the "war on drugs" equated to a form of institutional racism.[2] In *The New Jim Crow* though, Alexander took the distinctive, bold step of arguing that a caste system based on race had endured in the United States, perpetuated by the war on drugs.

Looking at the legal system as a whole, Alexander concluded that mass incarceration involved a larger web of laws, policies, and informal customs. Mass incarceration, she wrote, "is a system that locks people not only behind actual bars in actual prisons, but also behind virtual

> **"** *The New Jim Crow* is an instant classic because it captures the emerging spirit of our age. For too long, there has been no mass fight back against the multileveled assault on poor and vulnerable people ... *The New Jim Crow* is a grand wake-up call in the midst of a long slumber of indifference to the poor and vulnerable. **"**
>
> Cornel West, "Foreword" to *The New Jim Crow: Mass Incarceration in the Age of Colorblindness*

bars and virtual walls."[3] While previous critics of the criminal justice system had focused on the tremendous growth in the number of Americans behind bars, Alexander showed how the system of social control did not end there. Additional millions of Americans found themselves caught in a web of legalized discrimination and political disenfranchisement, even after their release—and excluded from many economic opportunities because of their drug-related convictions.

Achievement in Context

The historical context surrounding *The New Jim Crow* shaped Alexander's approach to the topic of mass incarceration. In the book's opening pages, she shares an anecdote from the night of the 2008 US presidential election. She describes being "beyond thrilled" by Barack Obama's victory, but then leaving an election-night party and seeing a black man "on his knees in the gutter, hands cuffed behind his back, as several officers stood around him talking, joking, and ignoring his human existence."[4] The incident gave her an immediate and unpleasant reminder that racial inequalities could and would persist in the criminal justice system, even with the election of America's first black president.

Indeed, the Obama administration mostly continued the same policies of policing the drug war that previous administrations had implemented. After his election, President Obama added $2 billion in funding for the Byrne grants* program, created in the 1980s by the administration of President Ronald Reagan* to help specialized narcotic task forces buy military equipment with federal aid.[5] The war on drugs and the militarization of America's police force continue to receive bipartisan support. *The New Jim Crow* illuminated a persistent system of racial inequality, obscured by the highly visible success of extraordinary black individuals in a colorblind* society. In the words of the philosophy scholar Cornel West:* "While the age of Obama is a time of historic breakthroughs at the level of racial symbols and political surfaces, Michelle Alexander's magisterial work takes us beyond these breakthroughs to the systemic breakdown of black and poor communities devastated by mass unemployment, social neglect, economic abandonment, and intense police surveillance."[6]

Limitations

James Forman Jr.,* a professor of law at Yale University, presented an all-encompassing critique of *The New Jim Crow*, suggesting that Alexander created an overblown comparison between Jim Crow and mass incarceration.[7] In the fifth chapter of *The New Jim Crow*, Alexander acknowledges the limits of her analogy. The first difference she discusses is the absence of overt racial hostility. Instead, "Racial violence has been rationalized, legitimated, and channeled through our criminal justice system; it is expressed as police brutality, solitary confinement, and the discriminatory and arbitrary imposition of the death penalty."[8] Thus the racism behind mass incarceration is more systemic and less personal than in Jim Crow.

A second limit involves the white people also ensnared by the war on drugs and mass incarceration, though at disproportionately lower rates. The formal colorblindness of mass incarceration distinguishes it from the previous racial caste systems. Alexander points out that "the inclusion of some white people in the system of control is essential to preserving the image of a colorblind criminal justice system and maintaining our self-image as fair and unbiased people."[9] The Civil Rights Movement's* triumph over Jim Crow ensured that the next caste system would have to be race-neutral in language and colorblind under the law—or at least appear so.

Finally, Alexander recognizes that some support exists in black communities for "get tough" policies. Yet overall, she says, surveys show that African Americans are less likely than white people to support harsh criminal justice policies.[10] Alexander compares the black people who support mass incarceration and the drug war to previous generations that found a measure of support under Jim Crow and slavery. She asserts, "The notion that black people have always been united in opposition to American caste systems is sheer myth."[11]

NOTES

1   Jennifer Schuessler, "Drug Policy as Race Policy: Best Seller Galvanizes the Debate," *New York Times* (March 6, 2012).

2   Michael H. Tonry, *Malign Neglect: Race, Crime, and Punishment in America* (New York: Oxford University Press, 1995); Jerome G. Miller, *Search and Destroy: African-American Males in the Criminal Justice System* (New York: Cambridge University Press, 1996); Marc Mauer, *Race to Incarcerate* (New York: New Press, 1999); Angela Y. Davis, *Are Prisons Obsolete?* (New York: Seven Stories Press, 2003).

3   Michelle Alexander, *The New Jim Crow: Mass Incarceration in the Age of Colorblindness* (New York: New Press), 12.

4   Alexander, *The New Jim Crow*, 2.

5   Alexander, *The New Jim Crow*, 84.

6   Cornel West, foreword to *The New Jim Crow: Mass Incarceration in the Age of Colorblindness*, by Michelle Alexander (New York: New Press, 2010), ix–x.

7   James Forman Jr., "Racial Critiques of Mass Incarceration: Beyond the New Jim Crow," *New York University Law Review* 87, no. 1 (2012): 101–46.

8   Alexander, *The New Jim Crow*, 202.

9   Alexander, *The New Jim Crow*, 204–5.

10 Alexander, *The New Jim Crow*, 208.

11 Alexander, *The New Jim Crow*, 211.

PLACE IN THE AUTHOR'S WORK

KEY POINTS

- As a civil rights* lawyer, Michelle Alexander has spent her career fighting for social justice.

- Although *The New Jim Crow* is Alexander's only book, she has become an important figure in new movements for racial justice.

- *The New Jim Crow* grew out of a change in Alexander's legal work—her concerns shifted from affirmative action* to the criminal justice system.

Positioning

In the opening pages of *The New Jim Crow: Mass Incarceration in the Age of Colorblindness*, Michelle Alexander recalls how she first encountered the comparison between mass incarceration* and segregation,* more than a decade before the book's 2010 publication. One day, she passed a sign stapled to a telephone pole that read "THE DRUG WAR IS THE NEW JIM CROW."* Alexander says that her initial reaction was skeptical—it was a flyer for a radical activist group meeting in a small community church. She recalled thinking that the analogy between the drug war and Jim Crow was "absurd": "I sighed, and muttered to myself something like, 'Yeah, the criminal justice system is racist in many ways, but it really doesn't help to make such an absurd comparison. People will think you're crazy.'"[1]

Alexander had started serving as director of the Racial Justice Project of the American Civil Liberties Union (ACLU)* in Northern California. She believed that although problems of racial bias plagued the criminal justice system, it was not any different from other major

> ❝ When I first joined the ACLU, no one imagined that the Racial Justice Project would focus its attention on criminal justice reform. The ACLU was engaged in important criminal justice work, but no one suspected that work would eventually become central to the agenda of the Racial Justice Project. The assumption was that the project would concentrate its efforts on defending affirmative action. ❞
>
> Michelle Alexander, *The New Jim Crow: Mass Incarceration in the Age of Colorblindness*

American institutions—a perspective typical among her colleagues in the legal profession and civil rights advocacy, for whom the pressing challenges of the time were to protect affirmative action (special consideration for women and minorities in education and employment) and to eradicate overt racism. During her tenure at the ACLU, Alexander shifted her focus from employment discrimination to the criminal justice system. She had come to a new realization, which would culminate with *The New Jim Crow*: "The activists who posted the sign on the telephone pole were not crazy; nor were the smattering of lawyers and advocates around the country who were beginning to connect the dots between our current system of mass incarceration and earlier forms of social control."[2]

Integration

After publishing *The New Jim Crow* in 2010, Alexander continued to examine the policies of the administration of President Barack Obama* toward mass incarceration and the war on the drug trade. By late that year, the chorus of voices calling for criminal justice reform and ending the "war" had even come to include conservative think tanks such as the Washington, DC-based Heritage Foundation.* The escalating costs of mass incarceration in a time of growing budget deficits had begun to rankle some fiscal conservatives. "Could this be the beginning of the end of the drug war?"[3] Alexander asked—yet on reviewing the Obama administration's policies, she concluded it was not; the drug war had become ingrained in the political and economic structure of the United States, serving as a proxy for social control over people of color.[4]

In 2013, Alexander wrote an article to commemorate the 50-year anniversary of the March on Washington* led by Rev. Martin Luther King Jr.,* one of the most important figures in the Civil Rights Movement.* She reflected on King's ability to see the links between racism and militarism, or "the connections between the wars we wage abroad and the utter indifference we have for poor people and people of color at home."[5] Alexander vowed to expand the scope of her analysis—in America's wars on drugs and terrorism, she saw it essential to understand the connection between systemic racism* and state power. She reiterated her earlier argument: ending mass incarceration would prove insufficient until political and social leaders abolished the underlying racial caste system.*

Significance

The New Jim Crow immediately established Alexander as a central figure in the struggle against mass incarceration and racial injustice in the United States. In 2013, she described her activities in the years after *The New Jim Crow* was published: "I have spent countless hours speaking in public forums—from universities, to prisons, to churches, to legal conferences, to community centers and beyond—about the birth of a new system of racial and social control, a penal system that would surely have Dr. Martin Luther King Jr. turning over in his grave. I have written and spoken about little else."[6]

The New Jim Crow helped make mass incarceration a core issue for a new generation of racial justice advocates and Alexander became a significant figure and spokesperson in this movement.

The New Jim Crow established Alexander's reputation as a significant figure among scholars of criminal justice and activists for racial justice. But perhaps more importantly, it has also become influential as protests against racial inequality and police brutality have increased and intensified across the United States.

In early 2015, Alexander wrote about her involvement with this social movement: "In recent months, I have marched in the streets with young people who have carried signs saying what shouldn't have to be said: Black Lives Matter. The words are urgent and necessary as we struggle to comprehend how our criminal justice system could deliver so little that looks or feels anything like justice for poor people and people of color, especially for young black men."[7]

NOTES

1   Michelle Alexander, *The New Jim Crow: Mass Incarceration in the Age of Colorblindness* (New York: New Press, 2010), 3.

2   Alexander, *The New Jim Crow*, 4.

3   Michelle Alexander, "Obama's Drug War," *The Nation* (December 9, 2010).

4   Alexander, "Obama's Drug War."

5   Michelle Alexander, "Breaking My Silence," *The Nation* (September 4. 2013).

6   Alexander, "Breaking My Silence."

7   Michelle Alexander, foreword to the Schott 50-State Report on Public Education and Black Males, accessed November 21, 2015, http://blackboysreport.org/national-summary/foreword/#.

SECTION 3
IMPACT

MODULE 9
THE FIRST RESPONSES

KEY POINTS

- The most significant criticisms of *The New Jim Crow* are that it neglects violent crime, the black community's support for tougher policing, and the incarceration of white people in the "war on drugs."*

- Michelle Alexander anticipated all these criticisms by disproving the significance of violent crime, clarifying the meaning of opinion polls in the black community, and insisting that the "war" on the drug trade is racially motivated despite its seeming colorblindness.*

- The overwhelmingly positive reception of *The New Jim Crow* has been shaped by the context of growing movements against systemic racism* and police brutality.

Criticism

Immediately after its publication, Michelle Alexander's *The New Jim Crow: Mass Incarceration in the Age of Colorblindness* was praised in many venues. The *New York Times Book Review* noted the book's extraordinary reach and influence: "Now and then a book comes along that might in time touch the public and educate social commentators, policymakers, and politicians about a glaring wrong that we have been living with that we also somehow don't know how to face."[1] Praise for *The New Jim Crow* even came from the conservative contributor Bill Frezza at *Forbes*: "Once in a great while a writer at the opposite end of the political spectrum gets you to look at a familiar set of facts in a new way. Disconcerting as it is, you can feel your foundation shift as your mind struggles to reconcile this new point of view with long held beliefs."[2]

> ❝ The book marshals pages of statistics and legal citations to argue that the get-tough approach to crime that began in the Nixon* administration and intensified with Ronald Reagan's declaration of the war on drugs has devastated black America …That is a familiar argument made by many critics of the criminal justice system, but Professor Alexander's book goes further, asserting that the crackdown was less a response to the actual explosion of violent crime than a deliberate effort to push back the gains of the civil rights* movement. ❞
>
> Jessica Schuessler, *New York Times*

Among Alexander's critics, the Yale Law School professor James Forman Jr.* expressed the most pronounced reservations. While he recognizes the book's accomplishments and significance, he outlines three points of criticism. First, he maintains that Alexander fails to discuss violent crime and overestimates the drug war's impact in mass incarceration.* Next, she downplays the support within black communities for increased policing and harsher sentencing. Finally, in overlooking how the drug war also ensnares white people, she overstates the role of race and neglects the class inequalities of mass incarceration.[3]

Responses

While Alexander is sharply critical of the notion that violent crime necessitates mass incarceration, James Forman Jr. points out that homicide and robbery rates rose sharply in the decades before President Reagan's* war on drugs. He feels Alexander underplays how violence and street crime increased incarceration rates and made voters receptive to tough-talking politicians. For her own part, Alexander counters that incarceration continued to rise long after violent crime numbers had begun to fall. "As many researchers have shown," Alexander explains, "violent crime rates have fluctuated over the years and bear little relationship to incarceration rates."[4]

Alexander anticipated Forman Jr.'s other criticisms in the fifth chapter of *The New Jim Crow*, where she addressed the limits of the segregation*–incarceration analogy. She recognizes that many African Americans supported "get tough" policies, making the war on drugs distinct from Jim Crow*—but also maintains that the extent of this support is often overstated. Alexander argues that African Americans will back harsher punishment if the only other option is rampant crime, but surveys indicate much greater support for alternatives such as job creation and educational reform.[5] Alexander also acknowledges that the victims of the drug war are not exclusively black, but insists that this does not make it any less motivated by racial concerns: "The fact that white people are harmed by the drug war does not mean they are the real targets, the designated enemy … Black and brown people are the principal targets in this war; white people are collateral damage."[6]

Conflict and Consensus

The New Jim Crow made an indelible, immediate impact and quickly became one of the most influential books of its time. Despite an initial hardcover printing of only 3,000 in 2010, it spent six weeks on the *New York Times* paperback nonfiction best seller list, with sales totaling 175,000 by March 2012.[7] Even the book's fiercest critic, James Foreman Jr., recognized the magnitude of Alexander's accomplishment: "By skillfully deploying a rhetorically provocative claim, she has drawn significant media attention to the often ignored phenomenon of mass imprisonment."[8]

In the context of emerging movements against police brutality, the drug war and mass incarceration, it seems likely that the influence of *The New Jim Crow* will grow. Previously published works had already exposed the racial biases behind so many of America's "get tough" policies on crime and drugs. *The New Jim Crow*, however, appeared at a time of increasing assertiveness among a new generation of African American activists—and to some extent the book has also fueled these movements. As the African American thinker Cornel West* put it: "Once you read it, you have crossed the Rubicon and there is no return to sleepwalking. You are now awakened to a dark and ugly reality that has been in place for decades and that is continuous with the racist underside of American history from the advent of slavery onward."[9]

NOTES

1   Jessica Schuessler, "Drug Policy as Race Policy: Best Seller Galvanizes the Debate," *New York Times* (March 6, 2012).

2   Bill Frezza, "Is Drug War Driven Mass Incarceration the New Jim Crow?" *Forbes* (February 28, 2012).

3   James Forman Jr., "Racial Critiques of Mass Incarceration: Beyond the New Jim Crow," *New York University Law Review* 87, no. 1 (2012): 101–46.

4   Michelle Alexander, *The New Jim Crow: Mass Incarceration in the Age of Colorblindness* (New York: New Press, 2010), 101.

5   Alexander, *The New Jim Crow*, 208.

6   Alexander, *The New Jim Crow*, 205.

7   Schuessler, "Drug Policy as Race Policy."

8   Forman Jr., "Racial Critiques of Mass Incarceration," 112.

9   Cornel West, foreword to *The New Jim Crow: Mass Incarceration in the Age of Colorblindness* (New York: New Press, 2010), x.

MODULE 10
THE EVOLVING DEBATE

KEY POINTS

- While a number of scholars and advocates had previously published critical analyses of the systemic racism* in mass incarceration,* The New Jim Crow enjoys widespread exposure and influence.

- *The New Jim Crow* has influenced subsequent studies by criminologists* and legal scholars, but has made its greatest impact among a younger generation of activists for racial justice.

- *The New Jim Crow* has already begun to shape policy debates and calls for reform, and its impact may grow as mass incarceration and the drug war are held to greater scrutiny by society at large.

Uses and Problems

The publication of Michelle Alexander's *The New Jim Crow: Mass Incarceration in the Age of Colorblindness* followed years of research and criticism by scholars and activists investigating the issue. In 1986—at the onset of the "war on drugs" declared by the administration of President Reagan*—The Sentencing Project* was founded to highlight inequalities and alarming trends in the criminal justice system by focusing on research, media campaigns, and advocacy for policy reform.[1] The research of The Sentencing Project and its executive director, Marc Mauer,* was presented in the 1999 book *Race to Incarcerate*.[2] In 2013, this influential work was redesigned as an illustrated book aimed at younger readers, and Michelle Alexander was asked to write the foreword. She recalled that while writing *The New Jim Crow*, her copy of *Race to Incarcerate* "was so frayed that the cover was nearly falling off."[3]

> **❝** *The New Jim Crow*, Michelle Alexander's very influential work on the role of race in mass incarceration, has brought a new awareness of the deep roots and long history of large-scale racial disparities in US law enforcement and imprisonment. **❞**
>
> Ernest Drucker, *A Plague of Prisons: The Epidemiology of Mass Incarceration in America*

A field of critical scholarship on the criminal justice system had developed in the late 1990s, with especially influential works written by the criminologist Michael H. Tonry,* professor emerita of feminist studies at the University of California Angela Y. Davis,* and the journalist Christian Parenti.*[4] *The New Jim Crow*, however, has reached a larger audience and made a greater impact. As an unexpected best seller, the book sparked a wider conversation about mass incarceration in America. It has also gained influence among young activists and will likely shape future discussions of American racism.

Schools of Thought

Given the book's positive reception by scholars, significance for activists, and its media prominence, *The New Jim Crow* is likely to have a lasting impact. Numerous works of criminology and legal studies cite *The New Jim Crow*, particularly books by Ernest Drucker* (a scholar noted for his work on prison policy and society), the political scientist Marie Gottschalk,* and Jonathan Simon* (a scholar noted for his work on crime and society).[5] Additionally, *The New Jim Crow* may prove even more influential as it is adopted by a new generation of activists organizing social movements in response to police brutality and the systemic racism of the criminal justice system. These young activists are intent on challenging the racial inequalities perpetuated by American institutions, especially in the law-enforcement arena.

Using Alexander's book as a foundation, the group Veterans of Hope* has created two guides dedicated to ending mass incarceration. The study guide is meant to encourage dialogue about race, prisons, and the criminal justice system, while the organizing guide offers advice on movement-building and effective campaigns.[6] Michelle Alexander's influence caused her to be added—alongside Angela Y. Davis—to the advisory board of a prominent organization called Dream Defenders.* This group falls within the broader social movement known as Black Lives Matter,* which began in 2013 in response to a number of highly publicized police shootings of black men.

In Current Scholarship

The literature on mass incarceration continues to grow. Angela Y. Davis and the French sociologist* Loïc Wacquant* rank among the best-known scholars focused on understanding the links between race, class, and the criminal justice system. Davis, Wacquant, and the former death-row inmate and prison activist Mumia Abu-Jamal* contributed articles to a 2014 special issue of the journal *Socialism and Democracy*.[7] One enduring question in this issue and the scholarship at large concerns the significance of class and its relationship to race.

In his contribution to the 2014 issue of *Socialism and Democracy*, Wacquant continues to emphasize the role of class in what he calls "hyperincarceration,"* a term he proposes as a replacement for mass incarceration. In using it, Wacquant means that class trumps race: black people in prisons and the criminal justice system disproportionately come from the lower classes, whereas affluent black people are more likely to be left alone. Wacquant argues that a "surplus population" of young men growing up in jobless inner-city ghettos has been the main target of this system of exclusion and state control.[8] This population, he contends, was a byproduct of the economic doctrine of neoliberalism*—a staunchly conservative policy of deregulation of business and trade, privatization, and fiscal austerity. It was promoted in the 1980s by the likes of Ronald Reagan—who also oversaw the massive expansion of the war on drugs.

While Wacquant's argument places greater emphasis on class factors, he does not criticize or engage with Alexander's work directly. To be sure, clear differences exist in the emphasis of race and class in their arguments. However, both see the same core problem— the excessive incarceration of black people—as one that deserves far greater scrutiny and attention.

NOTES

1   The Sentencing Project, accessed November 24, 2015, http://www. sentencingproject.org/template/page.cfm?id=2.

2   Marc Mauer, *Race to Incarcerate* (New York: New Press, 1999).

3   Michelle Alexander, foreword to *Race to Incarcerate: A Graphic Retelling*, by Marc Mauer and Sabrina Jones (New York: The New Press, 2013), vii.

4   Michael H. Tonry, *Malign Neglect: Race, Crime, and Punishment in America* (New York: Oxford University Press, 1995); Angela Y. Davis, "Masked Racism: Reflections on the Prison Industrial Complex," *Colorlines* (September 10, 1998), accessed November 14, 2015, http://www. colorlines.com/articles/masked-racism-reflections-prison-industrial-complex; Christian Parenti, *Lockdown America: Police and Prisons in the Age of Crisis* (New York: Verso 1999).

5   Ernest Drucker, *A Plague of Prisons: The Epidemiology of Mass Incarceration in America* (New York: New Press, 2011); Marie Gottschalk, *Caught: The Prison State and the Lockdown of American Politics* (Princeton, NJ: Princeton University Press, 2015); Jonathan Simon, *Mass Incarceration on Trial: A Remarkable Court Decision and the Future of Prisons in America* (New York: New Press, 2014).

6   Chris Moore-Backman et al., *The New Jim Crow Study Guide and Call to Action* (Denver, CO: The Visions of Hope Project, 2013); Daniel Hunter, ed., *Building a Movement to End the New Jim Crow* (Denver, CO: The Visions of Hope Project, 2015).

7   Mumia Abu-Jamal and Johanna Fernández, "Locking Up Dissidents and
     Punishing the Poor: The Roots of Mass Incarceration," *Socialism and
     Democracy* 28, no. 3 (2014): 1–14; Angela Y. Davis, "Deepening the
     Debate over Mass Incarceration," Socialism and Democracy 28, no. 3
     (2014): 15–23; Loïc Wacquant, "Class, Race and Hyperincarceration in
     Revanchist America," Socialism and Democracy 28, no. 3 (2014): 35–56.

8   Wacquant, "Class, Race and Hyperincarceration in Revanchist America,"
     42–3.

MODULE 11
IMPACT AND INFLUENCE TODAY

KEY POINTS

- *The New Jim Crow* is an increasingly influential book, especially among people concerned with social justice and racial equality.

- Michelle Alexander presented a strong challenge to civil rights* organizations—she criticized their focus on older forms of explicit prejudice and their silence about the systemic racism* of mass incarceration.*

- Whereas some critics have charged that Alexander overstates the role of racism in mass incarceration, others have criticized her for primarily addressing an audience of liberal white professionals.

Position

With its intellectual and political impact, Michelle Alexander's *The New Jim Crow: Mass Incarceration in the Age of Colorblindness* is certainly a notable piece of recent scholarship. As a best seller, the book gained a reputation as essential reading for anyone concerned with racial justice. In 2015, for instance, Mark Zuckerberg,* the CEO of Facebook,* selected *The New Jim Crow* for his book club, which focuses on "big ideas that influence society and business." Zuckerberg explained, "I've been interested in learning about criminal justice reform for a while, and this book was highly recommended by several people I trust."[1]

As *The New Jim Crow* has achieved extraordinary success, mass incarceration has come under increasing scrutiny from policymakers—and calls for reform have come from both the left and right sides of the political spectrum. In an initial step toward

> **❝** This social justice book outlines the many ways the US criminal justice system discriminates against minorities, disadvantages them and prevents everyone from having equal opportunity. **❞**
>
> Mark Zuckerberg, Facebook CEO

sentencing reform, the Obama* administration announced in 2014 that it would consider requests for clemency from drug offenders.[2] The following year, the US Justice Department gave early releases to 6,000 drug offenders in federal prison and Obama became the first sitting president to visit a federal prison.[3] Demands for sentencing reform have also come from some conservatives, most notably the billionaire Koch brothers,* who have used their collective fortune to back a number of causes highly unpopular with liberals.[4] In this context of the growing criticism of mass incarceration, it is likely *The New Jim Crow* will continue to exert growing influence.

Interaction

Though Michelle Alexander did not directly criticize any single author or school of thought, she presented a radical challenge to civil rights organizations. She maintains that the civil rights community stayed silent about mass incarceration for decades. The stigma of criminality led many advocates to bypass the plight of young people of color ensnared by the "war on drugs."* Alexander herself was not especially concerned with the criminal justice system at the start of her career as a civil rights lawyer. She contends, "Challenging mass incarceration requires something civil rights activists have long been reluctant to do: advocacy on behalf of criminals."[5] She also asserts that a political consensus surrounding the crackdown on crime and drugs also extended to civil rights organizations. Alexander declares, "Those of us in the civil rights community are not immune to the racial stereotypes that pervade media imagery and political rhetoric; nor do we operate outside of the political context."[6]

In a more general sense, *The New Jim Crow* articulates an urgent need to recognize the systemic racism that developed since the United States became a legally colorblind* society. Alexander is critical of civil rights organizations that still mobilize mainly around "old-fashioned racism": "A new civil rights movement cannot be organized around the relics of the earlier system of control if it is to address meaningfully the racial realities of our time."[7] Alexander insists that racism no longer limits itself to an individual mentality of prejudice; it is increasingly institutionalized in acceptable forms of social control.

The Continuing Debate

The critique of *The New Jim Crow* by the Yale law professor James Forman Jr.* represents a perspective close to the liberal civil rights position that Alexander rejects. Forman Jr. is the son of a prominent civil rights activist, James Forman,* who was a central figure in the Student Non-Violent Coordinating Committee (SNCC),* an important body in the wider Civil Rights Movement,* during the early 1960s. He contends that Alexander's argument exaggerates how the drug war played a role in mass incarceration and the extent of institutional racism in the criminal justice system. For him, Alexander overstates her Jim Crow* analogy and emphasizes that white people were also incarcerated in the drug war—while many within the black community have supported tougher policing and sentencing.[8]

Other scholars have also criticized *The New Jim Crow* for being "whitewashed" and Alexander for appeasing an audience of liberal white professionals.[9] Greg Thomas,* an associate professor of global black studies, contends, "The actually implied audience of the text is a provincial white and middle-class audience for whom any anti-racist talk that is too Black or too radical is an abomination."[10] Joseph D.

Osel,* a scholar of psychology and politics, has voiced a similar argument: "There is no ... acknowledgment that the likely champions of the text are the direct and continued benefactors of the 'caste system' they so deplore."[11]

For all the persuasive power of her argument, then, Alexander did not make converts of every respected scholar studying the same issues.

NOTES

1   Richard Feloni, "Why Mark Zuckerberg Wants Everyone to Read 'The New Jim Crow,'" *Business Insider* (May 14, 2015).

2   Sari Horwitz, "Justice Department Prepares for Clemency Requests from Thousands of Inmates," *Washington Post* (April 21, 2014).

3   Sari Horwitz, "Justice Department Set to Free 6,000 Prisoners, Largest One-Time Release," *Washington Post* (October 6, 2015).

4   Sari Horwitz, "Unlikely Allies," *Washington Post* (August 15, 2015).

5   Michelle Alexander, *The New Jim Crow: Mass Incarceration in the Age of Colorblindness* (New York: NewPress, 2010), 226.

6   Alexander, *The New Jim Crow*, 224.

7   Alexander, *The New Jim Crow*, 222–3.

8   James Forman Jr., "Racial Critiques of Mass Incarceration: Beyond the New Jim Crow," *New York University Law Review* 87, no. 1 (2012), 101–46.

9   Joseph D. Osel, "Black Out: Michelle Alexander's Operational Whitewash: 'The New Jim Crow' Reviewed," *International Journal of Radical Critique* 1, no. 1 (2012); Greg Thomas, "Why Some Like The New Jim Crow So Much," accessed November 26, 2015, http://imixwhatilike.org/2012/04/26/whysomelikethenewjimcrowsomuch/.

10 Thomas, "Why Some Like The New Jim Crow So Much."

11 Osel, "Black Out."

WHERE NEXT?

KEY POINTS

- *The New Jim Crow* is likely to gain in influence as social movements become more vocal in their criticism of the criminal justice system in the United States.

- *The New Jim Crow* will make an enduring impact by revealing the institutional racism* behind mass incarceration.*

- While others wrote about mass incarceration before, Michelle Alexander took the radical step of comparing it with Jim Crow*—the segregationist* laws and customs enforced against black people in the Southern United States following slavery.

Potential

Michelle Alexander's *The New Jim Crow: Mass Incarceration in the Age of Colorblindness* will only grow in influence if racial equality advocates continue to amplify their calls for criminal justice reform. The grassroots movement known as Black Lives Matter* increased its visibility following the shooting death of an unarmed black teenager by a white police officer in Ferguson, Missouri during the summer of 2014. Numerous incidents under similar circumstances, often captured on video, have instigated the further growth of this movement. Protests have focused on police brutality, but these incidents have also exposed layers of corruption and racism that permeate the criminal justice system.

As the most significant movement for racial justice since the 1960s, Black Lives Matter has extended beyond police brutality to reveal multiple forms of institutional racism. The Stop Mass Incarceration

> ❝The social movement fanned and fueled by this historic book is a democratic awakening that says we do care, that the racial caste system must be dismantled, that we need a revolution in our warped priorities, a transfer of power from oligarchs to the people—and that we are willing to live and die to make it so! ❞
>
> Cornel West,* foreword to *The New Jim Crow: Mass Incarceration in the Age of Colorblindness*

Network (SMIN)* has also played a key role in organizing protests. It is "determined to bring forth a movement of millions of people, from all walks of life, in steadfast resistance to the New Jim Crow and we will not stop until mass incarceration and the police murder of Black, Latino and other oppressed peoples stops."[1] That this group explicitly references *The New Jim Crow* testifies to the book's influence in the movement.

After nearly 30 years of bipartisan consensus, more political figures are questioning the US government's ongoing "war on drugs"* and the explosive growth of America's penal population. Even those unconcerned with its injustices recognize that mass incarceration has become a tremendous fiscal burden.[2] However, Alexander warns that if the end of mass incarceration does not include a greater abolition of systemic racism, a new racial caste system* will reemerge.

Future Directions

Years before the publication of *The New Jim Crow*, numerous scholars and activists wrote about mass incarceration and the racism that fueled the war on drugs. Unless the criminal justice system undergoes fundamental reforms, future scholars and activists will likely continue to critically investigate every dimension of this broken system. This becomes more probable as some young people influenced by the Black Lives Matter movement enter the ranks of academia.

Even as the criminal justice system comes under greater scrutiny and the drug war becomes increasingly unpopular, Alexander cautions that any attempt to abolish mass incarceration will encounter strong resistance—a point she sharpens by identifying the various groups that have solidified economic and political interests in the system. She considers the possibility of reducing the incarceration rate to 1970s levels, a move that would require the release of 80 percent of America's prisoners. Yet politicians who use employment as a rallying point will almost certainly stand in the way.

"If four out of five people were released from prisons," she calculates, "far more than a million people could lose their jobs."[3] She also describes the capital investment in private prisons, which includes rich and powerful individuals such as former vice president Dick Cheney.* Alexander concludes, "They are deeply interested in expanding the market—increasing the supply of prisoners—not eliminating the pool of people who can be held captive for a profit."[4]

Summary
The New Jim Crow exposes entrenched institutional racism plaguing the criminal justice system and has become influential at a time when mass incarceration has come under increasing attack from a host of social movements. Alexander reveals how racism continues through the systemic actions of institutions, even in a society whose legal system is now officially colorblind. She places mass incarceration in historical context by comparing it with the segregation practices of Jim Crow— they represent two phases of what Alexander calls the racial caste system that disenfranchises black people. The main factor driving mass incarceration has been the war on drugs, which police have fought most intensely against people of color in inner-city neighborhoods. *The New Jim Crow* debunks the idea that the drug war is actually about crime or

drugs—rates of drug use were in fact declining when the Reagan* administration escalated enforcement efforts.

The New Jim Crow is likely to grow in appeal and importance as social movements step up their challenges to the criminal justice system. Others had previously investigated connections between racism, the drug war, and mass incarceration—but Alexander stood apart with her comparisons to Jim Crow. She revealed stark similarities between mass incarceration and segregation, both of which act as racial caste systems of exclusion and control; both also result in economic marginalization, political exclusion, and personal stigma. Alexander also shows the two as political reactions against the racial equality gains that preceded them.

As Jim Crow laws were passed in an effort to reverse the gains black Americans made during Reconstruction* (the period following the end of slavery and the American Civil War* of 1861–5), the war on drugs played a central role in the conservative backlash against the changes attained by the movements of the 1960s. In the years since Alexander's book, a powerful counteroffensive has emerged—spreading from the grassroots level to a point of national prominence as it calls for wholesale changes in America's criminal justice system. That leaders within this overarching movement cite Michelle Alexander's work as an influence points to how *The New Jim Crow* has achieved something remarkable: a rare leap from identifying a broken element of society to the initial stages of transforming it.

NOTES

1 Stop Mass Incarceration Network, accessed November 28, 2015, http:// stopmassincarceration.net/about/.

2 Sari Horwitz, "Unlikely Allies," Washington Post (August 15, 2015).

3 Michelle Alexander, *The New Jim Crow* (New York: New Press, 2010), 230.

4 Alexander, *The New Jim Crow*, 230.

GLOSSARY

GLOSSARY OF TERMS

Affirmative action: the practice of offering special consideration to racial minorities and women, particularly in matters of education and employment. The idea originated in the Reconstruction era (1865–77), but was mainly implemented after the Civil Rights Movement as a means of counteracting discrimination.

American Civil Liberties Union (ACLU): an organization created to defend the individual liberties and rights guaranteed by the US Constitution. Founded in 1920, its current membership is more than 500,000 and its annual budget is more than $130 million.

American Civil War (1861–5): a conflict that saw the army of the North fight the army of the slave-holding Southern states over the future of the Union, or United States of America; slavery, indeed, played a significant role in the ideological conflict that partially provoked the war.

Apartheid: a system of legally sanctioned racial segregation in South Africa from 1948 to 1994 that discriminated against black people.

Black Lives Matter: a social movement among African Americans to protest police brutality and racial inequalities in the criminal justice system. The phrase began as a hashtag on social media in 2013, following the acquittal of George Zimmerman in the death of unarmed black teenager Trayvon Martin.

Byrne grants: a program that provides federal aid to local law enforcement, particularly to fight the war on drugs. In some states, up to 90 percent of Byrne grant money is applied to specialized narcotics task forces.

Capitalism: an economic system based on private ownership of the means of production, and the pursuit of profit through the creation and circulation of goods and services. Its core characteristics are wage labor, market competition, and the accumulation of capital.

Civil rights: the rights that protect the freedoms of speech, worship, assembly, and privacy from infringement by government, organizations, or private individuals. These include protection from discrimination on the basis of race, ethnicity, gender, sexual orientation, religion, or disability.

Civil Rights Movement: the ensemble of social movements that organized to defeat Jim Crow forms of racial segregation in America's Southern states, roughly between 1955 and 1965.

Colorblindness: an ideology that denies the significance of race and the persistence of racial inequality. Whereas prior ideologies of racism were explicit in their discrimination, in the post-Civil Rights era the claim to not see race has become a means of ignoring and perpetuating racism.

Criminologist: scholar of criminal behavior and criminal law

Department of Housing and Urban Development (HUD): a cabinet department created by President Lyndon B. Johnson in 1965 as part of the "Great Society." Its mission is to create inclusive communities and quality affordable housing.

Dream Defenders: a community organization based in South Florida and connected with the Black Lives Matter movement. Their core demands are an end to police murders of people of color and the release of America's prison population of more than two million.

Facebook: an online social networking service with more than one billion users worldwide. The website was originally launched by a group of Harvard College undergraduates in 2004.

Grandfather clause: early twentieth-century legislation adopted in Southern states such as Alabama, Georgia, and Virginia. It gave white men the automatic right to vote without paying a poll tax or passing a literacy test, so long as a male ancestor had voted in the state prior to 1870.

The Heritage Foundation: a conservative think tank based in Washington, DC, which has played a significant role in shaping public policy, especially during Republican administrations. Its core principles are free enterprise, limited government, and strong national defense.

Hyperincarceration: a term coined by the French sociologist Loïc Wacquant as a refinement of mass incarceration. It emphasizes how poor black people, as opposed to middle-class or affluent African Americans, are disproportionately targeted by the criminal justice system.

Institutional (or "systemic") racism: the ways that racial disparities in education, healthcare, employment, housing, criminal justice, and political power are perpetuated through impersonal methods. This differs from prior forms of racism based on explicit prejudice and direct discrimination.

Jim Crow: the name for state and local laws in the Southern states that enforced racial segregation and the disenfranchisement of African Americans after Reconstruction. Originally, "Jim Crow" was the name of a popular song-and-dance routine that caricatured black people in minstrel shows.

Mandatory minimum sentencing: a court decision that limits judicial discretion by mandating that people convicted of certain crimes must serve a minimum length of time in person. New mandatory minimums were enacted in the war on drugs during the 1980s, in particular creating differences in sentencing for crack cocaine versus powder cocaine.

March on Washington: a massive rally attended by 250,000 in Washington, DC on August 27, 1963. The demands of the march were for jobs and freedom for African Americans. It was a crucial event in the Civil Rights Movement, mainly known for Martin Luther King's "I Have A Dream" speech.

Marxism: the economic, historical, and social analysis of the German political philosopher Karl Marx (1818–83). For Marx, conflict between classes, notably those who labor and those who profit from that labor, is the principal driver of history. Marxist thought greatly influenced the communist movement of the twentieth century, and his wider analysis is considered important to many academic fields.

Mass incarceration: the tremendous increase of imprisonment in the United States, which has the world's largest penal population with more than two million people behind bars. The war on drugs has been a key factor driving mass incarceration.

McCleskey v. Kemp: a case argued before the US Supreme court in 1986–7 that challenged the death penalty on the grounds that it was imposed more than four times as often in murder cases involving black perpetrators and white victims. The Court ruled against charges of unequal treatment by a 5–4 vote.

National Association for the Advancement of Colored People (NAACP): an African American civil rights organization founded in 1909 for the purpose of attaining racial equality, particularly under the law. Its membership is approximately 300,000 and its annual budget is more than $27 million.

Neoliberalism: the resurgence of nineteenth-century ideas about laissez-faire capitalism, free trade, deregulation, privatization, and fiscal austerity. Neoliberal policies have been implemented in many parts of the world since the 1970s, with the political leaders Ronald Reagan of the United States and Margaret Thatcher of the United Kingdom being two of neoliberalism's fiercest advocates.

Poll tax: a tax levied during the Jim Crow era in Southern states as a prerequisite for registering to vote.

Prison–industrial complex: a term that compares the interlocking economic and political interests behind mass incarceration with the military-industrial complex of the Cold War. It is a term often invoked by advocates for social justice, most prominently Angela Y. Davis.

Racial caste system: the notion that racial inequality in the United States functions like a caste system based on laws, customs, and practices of exclusion and control. Michelle Alexander argues that slavery, segregation, and mass incarceration are three historical phases of the racial caste system.

Racial profiling: the practices of police and other authorities that target people of a certain race based on prejudicial stereotypes. These practices have played a crucial role in perpetuating the racial inequalities of the criminal justice system.

Reconstruction: the federal government's efforts to transform the Southern states after the Civil War. Reconstruction entailed numerous attempts to protect the freedom of African Americans. The Republican Party abandoned this effort in a compromise surrounding the election of 1876, thus enabling white Southern elites to impose a new system of Jim Crow segregation.

Segregation: the separation of people according to racial or ethnic groups, which may apply to public accommodation, residential location, political participation, educational institutions, and the workplace. The segregation of blacks from whites was in effect in most of the United States through the early twentieth century, and in the American South until the 1960s.

Soros Justice Fellowship: funds made available to individuals working on projects that advance reform and spur debate about issues surrounding the US criminal justice system. The fellowship is administered by the Open Society Foundation created by billionaire philanthropist George Soros.

The Sentencing Project: a nonprofit organization founded in 1986 to promote sentencing reform, offer alternatives to incarceration, and eliminate racial disparities in the US criminal justice system.

Sociologist: a scholar of social structures and social behavior.

Stop Mass Incarceration Network (SMIN): an organization founded by Cornel West and Carl Dix in 2011, which has become a significant part of the African American movement against growing imprisonment and police brutality.

Student Non-Violent Coordinating Committee (SNCC): a crucial organization of the Civil Rights Movement founded in 1960, in the wake of sit-ins by college students to protest segregation. SNCC later adopted a more militant stance in leading the movement for "black power."

Veterans of Hope Project: an educational initiative founded in 1997 to promote forms of social activism based on spiritual faith. The project's founders, Vincent and Rosemarie Freeney Harding, are longtime activists who were involved with the Civil Rights Movement in the 1960s.

War on drugs: the efforts of the US government—initially under the Nixon administration but on a much larger scale in the Reagan administration—to crack down on drug use and sales through increased policing and harsher sentencing. The war on drugs has been a leading factor in the tremendous growth of the American penal population.

PEOPLE MENTIONED IN THE TEXT

Mumia Abu-Jamal (b. 1954) is an African American activist and journalist sentenced to death in 1982 for the murder of a police officer in Philadelphia, though his sentence was later changed to life imprisonment. He has written numerous books and articles about prison and the criminal justice system.

Harry A. Blackmun (1908–99) was an Associate Justice who served on the US Supreme Court from 1970 to 1994. He is best known as the author of the Court's majority opinion in the landmark abortion case Roe v. Wade.

Dick Cheney (b. 1941) was vice president of the United States, in office from 2001 to 2009. He was first elected to the US House of Representatives in 1978, and he served as secretary of defense from 1989 to 1993.

Todd R. Clear is provost and the former dean of the School of Criminal Justice at Rutgers University-Newark. He is the author of 13 books and the founding editor of the journal *Criminology & Public Policy*.

Bill Clinton (b. 1946) was the 42nd president of the United States, in office from 1993 to 2001. He previously served as governor of Arkansas from 1979 to 1981 and 1983 to 1992.

Elliot Currie (b. 1942) is professor of criminology, law and society at the University of California, Irvine.

Angela Y. Davis (b. 1944) is professor emerita of feminist studies at the University of California, Santa Cruz, and the author of several books about race, class, and gender. As an activist involved with the Black Panther Party and the Communist Party, she made the list of the FBI's Ten Most Wanted Fugitives in 1970.

Mike Davis (b. 1946) is distinguished professor of creative writing at the University of California, Riverside. He is best known for his books about social class, immigration, and the environment in Southern California, especially *City of Quartz* (1990) and *The Ecology of Fear* (1998).

Ernest Drucker is professor emeritus in the Department of Family and Social Medicine, Montefiore Medical Center/Albert Einstein College of Medicine, and senior research associate and scholar in residence at John Jay College of Criminal Justice. His research focuses on AIDS, prison, and drug policy.

W. E. B. Du Bois (1868–1963) was an African American sociologist and a pioneering civil rights activist. He was one of the co-founders of the NAACP and served as an editor for its journal, *The Crisis*. He was also a central figure in the early development of Pan-Africanism, and spent his final years living in Ghana.

James Forman (1928–2005) was a civil rights activist involved with the Student Non-Violent Coordinating Committee (SNCC) and the Black Panther Party during the 1960s. He spent his adult life teaching and organizing black and disenfranchised people to fight for social and economic equality.

James Forman Jr. (b. 1967) is a clinical professor of law at Yale Law School, and before that he taught at Georgetown Law from 2003 to 2011. His teaching and research focus on criminal procedure and criminal law policy, constitutional law, juvenile justice, and education law and policy.

Marie Gottschalk is professor of political science at the University of Pennsylvania. Her research interests include criminal justice, health policy, race, the development of the welfare state, and business–labor relations.

Randall Kennedy (b. 1954) is Michael R. Klein Professor of Law at Harvard University. He has written five books and numerous articles that address issues concerning American civil rights, race relations, and constitutional law.

Rev. Martin Luther King Jr. (1929–1968) was a leader of the Civil Rights Movement who used nonviolent civil disobedience to push for racial equality. In his final years, he became more critical of American militarism and organized struggles around class as well as race.

Charles Koch (b. 1935) is the chief executive officer of Koch Industries and, along with his brother David, a multi-billionaire who is among the richest people in the world. The Koch brothers are major financial supporters of conservative political organizations and think tanks that advocate for free-market economics.

David Koch (b. 1940) is executive vice president of Koch Industries. Along with his brother Charles, he is a major financial supporter of conservative political organizations and think tanks that advocate for free-market economics.

Marc Mauer is executive director of The Sentencing Project whose work specializes in issues surrounding race, sentencing policy, and the criminal justice system. He directs programs on criminal justice reform and has authored many influential publications and reports, including *Race to Incarcerate* (1999).

Jerome G. Miller (1931–2015) was a social worker who advocated for reforms in the juvenile and adult corrections systems. He is best known for leading the controversial shutdown of two juvenile reformatories in Massachusetts during the early 1970s.

Richard Nixon (1913–94) was the 37th president of the United States, in office from 1969 to 1974, and also vice president of the United States from 1953 to 1961. As a result of the Watergate scandal, he is the only president to have resigned from office.

Barack Obama (b. 1961), 44th president of the United States from 2009 to 2017, is the first African American to hold this office. He previously served as a US senator representing the state of Illinois from 2005 to 2009.

Joseph D. Osel is a critical theorist, writer, and editor who focuses on metaphysics and phenomenology, along with race relations and black history. He does research on anti-racism and resistance, and has written a collection of poetry.

Christian Parenti is an investigative journalist and a regular contributor to *The Nation*. He has reported from the wars in Iraq and Afghanistan and investigated the links between climate change and social unrest in various parts of the world.

Ronald Reagan (1911–2004) was the 40th president of the United States, in office from 1981 to 1989. Prior to his presidency, he was an actor and president of the Screen Actors Guild, and governor of California from 1967 to 1975.

Eric Schlosser (b. 1959) is an investigative journalist. He is most known for his exposé of the fast-food industry's unsanitary and discriminatory practices, which began as a two-part story in *Rolling Stone* and was eventually published in the book *Fast Food Nation*.

Jonathan Simon (b. 1959) is Adrian A. Kragen Professor of Law and director of the Center for the Study of Law and Society at the University of California, Berkeley. He has written numerous books that examine the role of crime and criminal justice in governing contemporary societies.

Greg Thomas is associate professor of African American literature at Tufts University. His scholarship concerns race and empire, global African literature, and body politics.

Michael H. Tonry is the McKnight Presidential Professor of Criminal Law and Policy and director of the Institute on Crime and Public Policy at the University of Minnesota. He has written or edited a number of books on the subjects of race, crime and punishment.

Loïc Wacquant (b. 1960) is professor of sociology at the University of California, Berkeley. His scholarly interests include race and class, urban marginality, and incarceration, and he has conducted fieldwork in urban jails in Brazil, France, and the United States.

Cornel West (b. 1953) is professor of philosophy and Christian practice at Union Theological Seminary and professor emeritus at Princeton University. He has written more than 20 books and is the one of the best-known African American public intellectuals.

Iris Marion Young (1949–2006) was professor of political science at the University of Chicago. Her work was concerned with contemporary political philosophy, feminist theory, and the ideals of justice and democracy.

Mark Zuckerberg (b. 1984) is the chairman and chief executive of Facebook, Inc., a social networking site that he cofounded. In 2015, his estimated personal wealth was $44.7 billion, making him the seventh richest American.

WORKS CITED

WORKS CITED

Abu-Jamal, Mumia, and Johanna Fernández. "Locking Up Dissidents and Punishing the Poor: The Roots of Mass Incarceration." *Socialism and Democracy* 28, no. 3 (2014): 1–14.

Alexander, Michelle. "Breaking My Silence." *The Nation*, September 4, 2013.

Foreword to *Race to Incarcerate: A Graphic Retelling*, by Marc Mauer and Sabrina Jones, vii–viii. New York: New Press, 2013.

Foreword to the Schott 50-State Report on Public Education and Black Males. Accessed November 21, 2015. http://blackboysreport.org/national-summary/foreword/#.

The New Jim Crow: Mass Incarceration in the Age of Colorblindness. New York: New Press, 2010.

"Obama's Drug War." *The Nation*, December 9, 2010.

Clear, Todd R. *Imprisoning Communities: How Mass Incarceration Makes Disadvantaged Neighborhoods Worse*. New York: NYU Press, 2009.

Cooper, Arnie. "America's Drug War Has Led to a 'New and Improved' Racial Caste System, Argues Michelle Alexander." *Vanderbilt Magazine*, December 2, 2013. Accessed December 22, 2015. http://news.vanderbilt.edu/vanderbiltmagazine/strong-convictions/.

Currie, Elliot. *Crime and Punishment in America*. New York: Metropolitan Books, 1998.

Davis, Angela Y. *Are Prisons Obsolete?* New York: Seven Stories Press, 2003.

"Deepening the Debate over Mass Incarceration." *Socialism and Democracy* 28, no. 3 (2014): 15–23.

"Masked Racism: Reflections on the Prison Industrial Complex." *Colorlines*, September 10, 1998. Accessed November 14, 2015. http://www.colorlines.com/articles/masked-racism-reflections-prison-industrial-complex.

Davis, Mike. "Hell Factories in the Field: A Prison-Industrial Complex." *The Nation*, February 20, 1995.

Drucker, Ernest. *A Plague of Prisons: The Epidemiology of Mass Incarceration in America*. New York: New Press, 2011.

Feloni, Richard. "Why Mark Zuckerberg Wants Everyone to Read 'The New Jim Crow.'" *Business Insider*, May 14, 2015.

Forman Jr., James. "Racial Critiques of Mass Incarceration: Beyond the New Jim Crow," *New York University Law Review* 87, no. 1 (2012): 101–46.

Frezza, Bill. "Is Drug War Driven Mass Incarceration the New Jim Crow?" *Forbes*, February 28, 2012.

Gottschalk, Marie. *Caught: The Prison State and the Lockdown of American Politics*. Princeton, NJ: Princeton University Press, 2015.

Horwitz, Sari. "Justice Department Prepares for Clemency Requests from Thousands of Inmates." *Washington Post*, April 21, 2014.

"Justice Department Set to Free 6,000 Prisoners, Largest One-Time Release." *Washington Post*, October 6, 2015.

"Unlikely Allies." *Washington Post*, August 15, 2015.

Hunter, Daniel, ed. *Building a Movement to End the New Jim Crow*. Denver, CO: The Visions of Hope Project, 2015.

Kennedy, Randall. *Race, Crime, and the Law*. New York: Pantheon Books, 1997.

Lott, Eric. *Love and Theft: Blackface and the American Minstrelsy*. New York: Oxford University Press, 1993.

Mauer, Marc. *Race to Incarcerate*. New York: New Press, 1999.

Miller, Jerome G. *Search and Destroy: African-American Males in the Criminal Justice System*. New York: Cambridge University Press, 1996.

Moore-Backman, Chris, et al. *The New Jim Crow Study Guide and Call to Action*. Denver, CO: The Visions of Hope Project, 2013.

Osel, Joseph D. "Black Out: Michelle Alexander's Operational Whitewash: 'The New Jim Crow' Reviewed." *International Journal of Radical Critique* 1, no. 1 (2012). Accessed November 26, 2015. http://philpapers.org/archive/OSEBOM.

Parenti, Christian. *Lockdown America: Police and Prison in the Age of Crisis* New York: Verso, 1999.

Schlosser, Eric. "The Prison-Industrial Complex." *The Atlantic*, December 1998.

Schuessler, Jennifer. "Drug Policy as Race Policy: Best Seller Galvanizes the Debate." *New York Times*, March 6, 2012.

Simon, Jonathan. *Mass Incarceration on Trial: A Remarkable Court Decision and the Future of Prisons in America*. New York: New Press, 2014.

Thomas, Greg. "Why Some Like The New Jim Crow So Much." Accessed November 26, 2015. http://imixwhatilike.org/2012/04/26/whysomelikethenewjimcrowsomuch/.

Tonry, Michael H. *Malign Neglect: Race, Crime, and Punishment in America*. New York: Oxford University Press, 1995.

Wacquant, Loïc. "Class, Race and Hyperincarceration in Revanchist America." *Socialism and Democracy* 28, no. 3 (2014): 35–56.

Prisons of Poverty. Minneapolis, MN: University of Minnesota Press, 2009.

West, Cornel. Foreword to *The New Jim Crow*, by Michelle Alexander, ix–xi. New York: New Press, 2010.

Young, Iris Marion. *Inclusion and Democracy*. New York: Oxford University Press, 2000.

THE MACAT LIBRARY
BY DISCIPLINE

The Macat Library By Discipline

AFRICANA STUDIES

Chinua Achebe's *An Image of Africa: Racism in Conrad's Heart of Darkness*
W. E. B. Du Bois's *The Souls of Black Folk*
Zora Neale Huston's *Characteristics of Negro Expression*
Martin Luther King Jr's *Why We Can't Wait*
Toni Morrison's *Playing in the Dark: Whiteness in the American Literary Imagination*

ANTHROPOLOGY

Arjun Appadurai's *Modernity at Large: Cultural Dimensions of Globalisation*
Philippe Ariès's *Centuries of Childhood*
Franz Boas's *Race, Language and Culture*
Kim Chan & Renée Mauborgne's *Blue Ocean Strategy*
Jared Diamond's *Guns, Germs & Steel: the Fate of Human Societies*
Jared Diamond's *Collapse: How Societies Choose to Fail or Survive*
E. E. Evans-Pritchard's *Witchcraft, Oracles and Magic Among the Azande*
James Ferguson's *The Anti-Politics Machine*
Clifford Geertz's *The Interpretation of Cultures*
David Graeber's *Debt: the First 5000 Years*
Karen Ho's *Liquidated: An Ethnography of Wall Street*
Geert Hofstede's *Culture's Consequences: Comparing Values, Behaviors, Institutes and Organizations across Nations*
Claude Lévi-Strauss's *Structural Anthropology*
Jay Macleod's *Ain't No Makin' It: Aspirations and Attainment in a Low-Income Neighborhood*
Saba Mahmood's *The Politics of Piety: The Islamic Revival and the Feminist Subject*
Marcel Mauss's *The Gift*

BUSINESS

Jean Lave & Etienne Wenger's *Situated Learning*
Theodore Levitt's *Marketing Myopia*
Burton G. Malkiel's *A Random Walk Down Wall Street*
Douglas McGregor's *The Human Side of Enterprise*
Michael Porter's *Competitive Strategy: Creating and Sustaining Superior Performance*
John Kotter's *Leading Change*
C. K. Prahalad & Gary Hamel's *The Core Competence of the Corporation*

CRIMINOLOGY

Michelle Alexander's *The New Jim Crow: Mass Incarceration in the Age of Colorblindness*
Michael R. Gottfredson & Travis Hirschi's *A General Theory of Crime*
Richard Herrnstein & Charles A. Murray's *The Bell Curve: Intelligence and Class Structure in American Life*
Elizabeth Loftus's *Eyewitness Testimony*
Jay Macleod's *Ain't No Makin' It: Aspirations and Attainment in a Low-Income Neighborhood*
Philip Zimbardo's *The Lucifer Effect*

ECONOMICS

Janet Abu-Lughod's *Before European Hegemony*
Ha-Joon Chang's *Kicking Away the Ladder*
David Brion Davis's *The Problem of Slavery in the Age of Revolution*
Milton Friedman's *The Role of Monetary Policy*
Milton Friedman's *Capitalism and Freedom*
David Graeber's *Debt: the First 5000 Years*
Friedrich Hayek's *The Road to Serfdom*
Karen Ho's *Liquidated: An Ethnography of Wall Street*

John Maynard Keynes's *The General Theory of Employment, Interest and Money*
Charles P. Kindleberger's *Manias, Panics and Crashes*
Robert Lucas's *Why Doesn't Capital Flow from Rich to Poor Countries?*
Burton G. Malkiel's *A Random Walk Down Wall Street*
Thomas Robert Malthus's *An Essay on the Principle of Population*
Karl Marx's *Capital*
Thomas Piketty's *Capital in the Twenty-First Century*
Amartya Sen's *Development as Freedom*
Adam Smith's *The Wealth of Nations*
Nassim Nicholas Taleb's *The Black Swan: The Impact of the Highly Improbable*
Amos Tversky's & Daniel Kahneman's *Judgment under Uncertainty: Heuristics and Biases*
Mahbub Ul Haq's *Reflections on Human Development*
Max Weber's *The Protestant Ethic and the Spirit of Capitalism*

FEMINISM AND GENDER STUDIES

Judith Butler's *Gender Trouble*
Simone De Beauvoir's *The Second Sex*
Michel Foucault's *History of Sexuality*
Betty Friedan's *The Feminine Mystique*
Saba Mahmood's *The Politics of Piety: The Islamic Revival and the Feminist Subject*
Joan Wallach Scott's *Gender and the Politics of History*
Mary Wollstonecraft's *A Vindication of the Rights of Woman*
Virginia Woolf's *A Room of One's Own*

GEOGRAPHY

The Brundtland Report's *Our Common Future*
Rachel Carson's *Silent Spring*
Charles Darwin's *On the Origin of Species*
James Ferguson's *The Anti-Politics Machine*
Jane Jacobs's *The Death and Life of Great American Cities*
James Lovelock's *Gaia: A New Look at Life on Earth*
Amartya Sen's *Development as Freedom*
Mathis Wackernagel & William Rees's *Our Ecological Footprint*

HISTORY

Janet Abu-Lughod's *Before European Hegemony*
Benedict Anderson's *Imagined Communities*
Bernard Bailyn's *The Ideological Origins of the American Revolution*
Hanna Batatu's *The Old Social Classes And The Revolutionary Movements Of Iraq*
Christopher Browning's *Ordinary Men: Reserve Police Batallion 101 and the Final Solution in Poland*
Edmund Burke's *Reflections on the Revolution in France*
William Cronon's *Nature's Metropolis: Chicago And The Great West*
Alfred W. Crosby's *The Columbian Exchange*
Hamid Dabashi's *Iran: A People Interrupted*
David Brion Davis's *The Problem of Slavery in the Age of Revolution*
Nathalie Zemon Davis's *The Return of Martin Guerre*
Jared Diamond's *Guns, Germs & Steel: the Fate of Human Societies*
Frank Dikotter's *Mao's Great Famine*
John W Dower's *War Without Mercy: Race And Power In The Pacific War*
W. E. B. Du Bois's *The Souls of Black Folk*
Richard J. Evans's *In Defence of History*
Lucien Febvre's *The Problem of Unbelief in the 16th Century*
Sheila Fitzpatrick's *Everyday Stalinism*

The Macat Library By Discipline

Eric Foner's *Reconstruction: America's Unfinished Revolution, 1863-1877*
Michel Foucault's *Discipline and Punish*
Michel Foucault's *History of Sexuality*
Francis Fukuyama's *The End of History and the Last Man*
John Lewis Gaddis's *We Now Know: Rethinking Cold War History*
Ernest Gellner's *Nations and Nationalism*
Eugene Genovese's *Roll, Jordan, Roll: The World the Slaves Made*
Carlo Ginzburg's *The Night Battles*
Daniel Goldhagen's *Hitler's Willing Executioners*
Jack Goldstone's *Revolution and Rebellion in the Early Modern World*
Antonio Gramsci's *The Prison Notebooks*
Alexander Hamilton, John Jay & James Madison's *The Federalist Papers*
Christopher Hill's *The World Turned Upside Down*
Carole Hillenbrand's *The Crusades: Islamic Perspectives*
Thomas Hobbes's *Leviathan*
Eric Hobsbawm's *The Age Of Revolution*
John A. Hobson's *Imperialism: A Study*
Albert Hourani's *History of the Arab Peoples*
Samuel P. Huntington's *The Clash of Civilizations and the Remaking of World Order*
C. L. R. James's *The Black Jacobins*
Tony Judt's *Postwar: A History of Europe Since 1945*
Ernst Kantorowicz's *The King's Two Bodies: A Study in Medieval Political Theology*
Paul Kennedy's *The Rise and Fall of the Great Powers*
Ian Kershaw's *The "Hitler Myth": Image and Reality in the Third Reich*
John Maynard Keynes's *The General Theory of Employment, Interest and Money*
Charles P. Kindleberger's *Manias, Panics and Crashes*
Martin Luther King Jr's *Why We Can't Wait*
Henry Kissinger's *World Order: Reflections on the Character of Nations and the Course of History*
Thomas Kuhn's *The Structure of Scientific Revolutions*
Georges Lefebvre's *The Coming of the French Revolution*
John Locke's *Two Treatises of Government*
Niccolò Machiavelli's *The Prince*
Thomas Robert Malthus's *An Essay on the Principle of Population*
Mahmood Mamdani's *Citizen and Subject: Contemporary Africa And The Legacy Of Late Colonialism*
Karl Marx's *Capital*
Stanley Milgram's *Obedience to Authority*
John Stuart Mill's *On Liberty*
Thomas Paine's *Common Sense*
Thomas Paine's *Rights of Man*
Geoffrey Parker's *Global Crisis: War, Climate Change and Catastrophe in the Seventeenth Century*
Jonathan Riley-Smith's *The First Crusade and the Idea of Crusading*
Jean-Jacques Rousseau's *The Social Contract*
Joan Wallach Scott's *Gender and the Politics of History*
Theda Skocpol's *States and Social Revolutions*
Adam Smith's *The Wealth of Nations*
Timothy Snyder's *Bloodlands: Europe Between Hitler and Stalin*
Sun Tzu's *The Art of War*
Keith Thomas's *Religion and the Decline of Magic*
Thucydides's *The History of the Peloponnesian War*
Frederick Jackson Turner's *The Significance of the Frontier in American History*
Odd Arne Westad's *The Global Cold War: Third World Interventions And The Making Of Our Times*

LITERATURE

Chinua Achebe's *An Image of Africa: Racism in Conrad's Heart of Darkness*
Roland Barthes's *Mythologies*
Homi K. Bhabha's *The Location of Culture*
Judith Butler's *Gender Trouble*
Simone De Beauvoir's *The Second Sex*
Ferdinand De Saussure's *Course in General Linguistics*
T. S. Eliot's *The Sacred Wood: Essays on Poetry and Criticism*
Zora Neale Huston's *Characteristics of Negro Expression*
Toni Morrison's *Playing in the Dark: Whiteness in the American Literary Imagination*
Edward Said's *Orientalism*
Gayatri Chakravorty Spivak's *Can the Subaltern Speak?*
Mary Wollstonecraft's *A Vindication of the Rights of Women*
Virginia Woolf's *A Room of One's Own*

PHILOSOPHY

Elizabeth Anscombe's *Modern Moral Philosophy*
Hannah Arendt's *The Human Condition*
Aristotle's *Metaphysics*
Aristotle's *Nicomachean Ethics*
Edmund Gettier's *Is Justified True Belief Knowledge?*
Georg Wilhelm Friedrich Hegel's *Phenomenology of Spirit*
David Hume's *Dialogues Concerning Natural Religion*
David Hume's *The Enquiry for Human Understanding*
Immanuel Kant's *Religion within the Boundaries of Mere Reason*
Immanuel Kant's *Critique of Pure Reason*
Søren Kierkegaard's *The Sickness Unto Death*
Søren Kierkegaard's *Fear and Trembling*
C. S. Lewis's *The Abolition of Man*
Alasdair MacIntyre's *After Virtue*
Marcus Aurelius's *Meditations*
Friedrich Nietzsche's *On the Genealogy of Morality*
Friedrich Nietzsche's *Beyond Good and Evil*
Plato's *Republic*
Plato's *Symposium*
Jean-Jacques Rousseau's *The Social Contract*
Gilbert Ryle's *The Concept of Mind*
Baruch Spinoza's *Ethics*
Sun Tzu's *The Art of War*
Ludwig Wittgenstein's *Philosophical Investigations*

POLITICS

Benedict Anderson's *Imagined Communities*
Aristotle's *Politics*
Bernard Bailyn's *The Ideological Origins of the American Revolution*
Edmund Burke's *Reflections on the Revolution in France*
John C. Calhoun's *A Disquisition on Government*
Ha-Joon Chang's *Kicking Away the Ladder*
Hamid Dabashi's *Iran: A People Interrupted*
Hamid Dabashi's *Theology of Discontent: The Ideological Foundation of the Islamic Revolution in Iran*
Robert Dahl's *Democracy and its Critics*
Robert Dahl's *Who Governs?*
David Brion Davis's *The Problem of Slavery in the Age of Revolution*

The Macat Library By Discipline

Alexis De Tocqueville's *Democracy in America*
James Ferguson's *The Anti-Politics Machine*
Frank Dikotter's *Mao's Great Famine*
Sheila Fitzpatrick's *Everyday Stalinism*
Eric Foner's *Reconstruction: America's Unfinished Revolution, 1863-1877*
Milton Friedman's *Capitalism and Freedom*
Francis Fukuyama's *The End of History and the Last Man*
John Lewis Gaddis's *We Now Know: Rethinking Cold War History*
Ernest Gellner's *Nations and Nationalism*
David Graeber's *Debt: the First 5000 Years*
Antonio Gramsci's *The Prison Notebooks*
Alexander Hamilton, John Jay & James Madison's *The Federalist Papers*
Friedrich Hayek's *The Road to Serfdom*
Christopher Hill's *The World Turned Upside Down*
Thomas Hobbes's *Leviathan*
John A. Hobson's *Imperialism: A Study*
Samuel P. Huntington's *The Clash of Civilizations and the Remaking of World Order*
Tony Judt's *Postwar: A History of Europe Since 1945*
David C. Kang's *China Rising: Peace, Power and Order in East Asia*
Paul Kennedy's *The Rise and Fall of Great Powers*
Robert Keohane's *After Hegemony*
Martin Luther King Jr.'s *Why We Can't Wait*
Henry Kissinger's *World Order: Reflections on the Character of Nations and the Course of History*
John Locke's *Two Treatises of Government*
Niccolò Machiavelli's *The Prince*
Thomas Robert Malthus's *An Essay on the Principle of Population*
Mahmood Mamdani's *Citizen and Subject: Contemporary Africa And The Legacy Of Late Colonialism*
Karl Marx's *Capital*
John Stuart Mill's *On Liberty*
John Stuart Mill's *Utilitarianism*
Hans Morgenthau's *Politics Among Nations*
Thomas Paine's *Common Sense*
Thomas Paine's *Rights of Man*
Thomas Piketty's *Capital in the Twenty-First Century*
Robert D. Putman's *Bowling Alone*
John Rawls's *Theory of Justice*
Jean-Jacques Rousseau's *The Social Contract*
Theda Skocpol's *States and Social Revolutions*
Adam Smith's *The Wealth of Nations*
Sun Tzu's *The Art of War*
Henry David Thoreau's *Civil Disobedience*
Thucydides's *The History of the Peloponnesian War*
Kenneth Waltz's *Theory of International Politics*
Max Weber's *Politics as a Vocation*
Odd Arne Westad's *The Global Cold War: Third World Interventions And The Making Of Our Times*

POSTCOLONIAL STUDIES

Roland Barthes's *Mythologies*
Frantz Fanon's *Black Skin, White Masks*
Homi K. Bhabha's *The Location of Culture*
Gustavo Gutiérrez's *A Theology of Liberation*
Edward Said's *Orientalism*
Gayatri Chakravorty Spivak's *Can the Subaltern Speak?*

PSYCHOLOGY

Gordon Allport's *The Nature of Prejudice*
Alan Baddeley & Graham Hitch's *Aggression: A Social Learning Analysis*
Albert Bandura's *Aggression: A Social Learning Analysis*
Leon Festinger's *A Theory of Cognitive Dissonance*
Sigmund Freud's *The Interpretation of Dreams*
Betty Friedan's *The Feminine Mystique*
Michael R. Gottfredson & Travis Hirschi's *A General Theory of Crime*
Eric Hoffer's *The True Believer: Thoughts on the Nature of Mass Movements*
William James's *Principles of Psychology*
Elizabeth Loftus's *Eyewitness Testimony*
A. H. Maslow's *A Theory of Human Motivation*
Stanley Milgram's *Obedience to Authority*
Steven Pinker's *The Better Angels of Our Nature*
Oliver Sacks's *The Man Who Mistook His Wife For a Hat*
Richard Thaler & Cass Sunstein's *Nudge: Improving Decisions About Health, Wealth and Happiness*
Amos Tversky's *Judgment under Uncertainty: Heuristics and Biases*
Philip Zimbardo's *The Lucifer Effect*

SCIENCE

Rachel Carson's *Silent Spring*
William Cronon's *Nature's Metropolis: Chicago And The Great West*
Alfred W. Crosby's *The Columbian Exchange*
Charles Darwin's *On the Origin of Species*
Richard Dawkin's *The Selfish Gene*
Thomas Kuhn's *The Structure of Scientific Revolutions*
Geoffrey Parker's *Global Crisis: War, Climate Change and Catastrophe in the Seventeenth Century*
Mathis Wackernagel & William Rees's *Our Ecological Footprint*

SOCIOLOGY

Michelle Alexander's *The New Jim Crow: Mass Incarceration in the Age of Colorblindness*
Gordon Allport's *The Nature of Prejudice*
Albert Bandura's *Aggression: A Social Learning Analysis*
Hanna Batatu's *The Old Social Classes And The Revolutionary Movements Of Iraq*
Ha-Joon Chang's *Kicking Away the Ladder*
W. E. B. Du Bois's *The Souls of Black Folk*
Émile Durkheim's *On Suicide*
Frantz Fanon's *Black Skin, White Masks*
Frantz Fanon's *The Wretched of the Earth*
Eric Foner's *Reconstruction: America's Unfinished Revolution, 1863-1877*
Eugene Genovese's *Roll, Jordan, Roll: The World the Slaves Made*
Jack Goldstone's *Revolution and Rebellion in the Early Modern World*
Antonio Gramsci's *The Prison Notebooks*
Richard Herrnstein & Charles A Murray's *The Bell Curve: Intelligence and Class Structure in American Life*
Eric Hoffer's *The True Believer: Thoughts on the Nature of Mass Movements*
Jane Jacobs's *The Death and Life of Great American Cities*
Robert Lucas's *Why Doesn't Capital Flow from Rich to Poor Countries?*
Jay Macleod's *Ain't No Makin' It: Aspirations and Attainment in a Low Income Neighborhood*
Elaine May's *Homeward Bound: American Families in the Cold War Era*
Douglas McGregor's *The Human Side of Enterprise*
C. Wright Mills's *The Sociological Imagination*

The Macat Library By Discipline

Thomas Piketty's *Capital in the Twenty-First Century*
Robert D. Putman's *Bowling Alone*
David Riesman's *The Lonely Crowd: A Study of the Changing American Character*
Edward Said's *Orientalism*
Joan Wallach Scott's *Gender and the Politics of History*
Theda Skocpol's *States and Social Revolutions*
Max Weber's *The Protestant Ethic and the Spirit of Capitalism*

THEOLOGY

Augustine's *Confessions*
Benedict's *Rule of St Benedict*
Gustavo Gutiérrez's *A Theology of Liberation*
Carole Hillenbrand's *The Crusades: Islamic Perspectives*
David Hume's *Dialogues Concerning Natural Religion*
Immanuel Kant's *Religion within the Boundaries of Mere Reason*
Ernst Kantorowicz's *The King's Two Bodies: A Study in Medieval Political Theology*
Søren Kierkegaard's *The Sickness Unto Death*
C. S. Lewis's *The Abolition of Man*
Saba Mahmood's *The Politics of Piety: The Islamic Revival and the Feminist Subject*
Baruch Spinoza's *Ethics*
Keith Thomas's *Religion and the Decline of Magic*

COMING SOON

Chris Argyris's *The Individual and the Organisation*
Seyla Benhabib's *The Rights of Others*
Walter Benjamin's *The Work Of Art in the Age of Mechanical Reproduction*
John Berger's *Ways of Seeing*
Pierre Bourdieu's *Outline of a Theory of Practice*
Mary Douglas's *Purity and Danger*
Roland Dworkin's *Taking Rights Seriously*
James G. March's *Exploration and Exploitation in Organisational Learning*
Ikujiro Nonaka's *A Dynamic Theory of Organizational Knowledge Creation*
Griselda Pollock's *Vision and Difference*
Amartya Sen's *Inequality Re-Examined*
Susan Sontag's *On Photography*
Yasser Tabbaa's *The Transformation of Islamic Art*
Ludwig von Mises's *Theory of Money and Credit*

Macat Disciplines

Access the greatest ideas and thinkers across entire disciplines, including

Postcolonial Studies

Roland Barthes's *Mythologies*
Frantz Fanon's *Black Skin, White Masks*
Homi K. Bhabha's *The Location of Culture*
Gustavo Gutiérrez's *A Theology of Liberation*
Edward Said's *Orientalism*
Gayatri Chakravorty Spivak's *Can the Subaltern Speak?*

Macat analyses are available from all good bookshops and libraries.

Access hundreds of analyses through one, multimedia tool.

Macat Disciplines

Access the greatest ideas and thinkers across entire disciplines, including

AFRICANA STUDIES

Chinua Achebe's *An Image of Africa: Racism in Conrad's Heart of Darkness*

W. E. B. Du Bois's *The Souls of Black Folk*

Zora Neale Hurston's *Characteristics of Negro Expression*

Martin Luther King Jr.'s *Why We Can't Wait*

Toni Morrison's *Playing in the Dark: Whiteness in the American Literary Imagination*

Macat analyses are available from all good bookshops and libraries.

Access hundreds of analyses through one, multimedia tool.

Macat Disciplines

Access the greatest ideas and thinkers across entire disciplines, including

FEMINISM, GENDER AND QUEER STUDIES

Simone De Beauvoir's
The Second Sex

Michel Foucault's
History of Sexuality

Betty Friedan's
The Feminine Mystique

Saba Mahmood's
*The Politics of Piety:
The Islamic Revival and
the Feminist Subject*

Joan Wallach Scott's
*Gender and the
Politics of History*

Mary Wollstonecraft's
*A Vindication of the
Rights of Woman*

Virginia Woolf's
A Room of One's Own

Judith Butler's
Gender Trouble

Macat analyses are available from all good bookshops and libraries.

Access hundreds of analyses through one, multimedia tool.

Macat Disciplines

Access the greatest ideas and thinkers across entire disciplines, including

CRIMINOLOGY

Michelle Alexander's
The New Jim Crow: Mass Incarceration in the Age of Colorblindness

Michael R. Gottfredson & Travis Hirschi's
A General Theory of Crime

Elizabeth Loftus's
Eyewitness Testimony

Richard Herrnstein & Charles A. Murray's
The Bell Curve: Intelligence and Class Structure in American Life

Jay Macleod's
Ain't No Makin' It: Aspirations and Attainment in a Low-Income Neighborhood

Philip Zimbardo's
The Lucifer Effect

Macat Disciplines

Access the greatest ideas and thinkers across entire disciplines, including

INEQUALITY

Ha-Joon Chang's, *Kicking Away the Ladder*

David Graeber's, *Debt: The First 5000 Years*

Robert E. Lucas's, *Why Doesn't Capital Flow from Rich To Poor Countries?*

Thomas Piketty's, *Capital in the Twenty-First Century*

Amartya Sen's, *Inequality Re-Examined*

Mahbub Ul Haq's, *Reflections on Human Development*

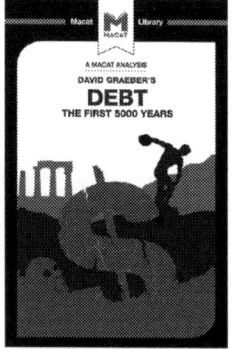

Macat analyses are available from all good bookshops and libraries.

Access hundreds of analyses through one, multimedia tool.

Join free for one month **library.macat.com**

Macat Disciplines

Access the greatest ideas and thinkers across entire disciplines, including

GLOBALIZATION

Arjun Appadurai's, *Modernity at Large: Cultural Dimensions of Globalisation*

James Ferguson's, *The Anti-Politics Machine*

Geert Hofstede's, *Culture's Consequences*

Amartya Sen's, *Development as Freedom*

Macat Disciplines

Access the greatest ideas and thinkers across entire disciplines, including

MAN AND THE ENVIRONMENT

The Brundtland Report's, *Our Common Future*
Rachel Carson's, *Silent Spring*
James Lovelock's, *Gaia: A New Look at Life on Earth*
Mathis Wackernagel & William Rees's, *Our Ecological Footprint*

Macat analyses are available from all good bookshops and libraries.

Access hundreds of analyses through one, multimedia tool.

Macat Disciplines

Access the greatest ideas and thinkers across entire disciplines, including

THE FUTURE OF DEMOCRACY

Robert A. Dahl's, *Democracy and Its Critics*
Robert A. Dahl's, *Who Governs?*
Alexis De Toqueville's, *Democracy in America*
Niccolò Machiavelli's, *The Prince*
John Stuart Mill's, *On Liberty*
Robert D. Putnam's, *Bowling Alone*
Jean-Jacques Rousseau's, *The Social Contract*
Henry David Thoreau's, *Civil Disobedience*

Macat Disciplines

Access the greatest ideas and thinkers across entire disciplines, including

TOTALITARIANISM

Sheila Fitzpatrick's, *Everyday Stalinism*
Ian Kershaw's, *The "Hitler Myth"*
Timothy Snyder's, *Bloodlands*

Macat analyses are available from all good bookshops and libraries.

Access hundreds of analyses through one, multimedia tool.
Join free for one month **library.macat.com**

Macat Pairs

Analyse historical and modern issues from opposite sides of an argument. Pairs include:

RACE AND IDENTITY

Zora Neale Hurston's
Characteristics of Negro Expression

Using material collected on anthropological expeditions to the South, Zora Neale Hurston explains how expression in African American culture in the early twentieth century departs from the art of white America. At the time, African American art was often criticized for copying white culture. For Hurston, this criticism misunderstood how art works. European tradition views art as something fixed. But Hurston describes a creative process that is alive, ever-changing, and largely improvisational. She maintains that African American art works through a process called 'mimicry'—where an imitated object or verbal pattern, for example, is reshaped and altered until it becomes something new, novel—and worthy of attention.

Frantz Fanon's
Black Skin, White Masks

Black Skin, White Masks offers a radical analysis of the psychological effects of colonization on the colonized.

Fanon witnessed the effects of colonization first hand both in his birthplace, Martinique, and again later in life when he worked as a psychiatrist in another French colony, Algeria. His text is uncompromising in form and argument. He dissects the dehumanizing effects of colonialism, arguing that it destroys the native sense of identity, forcing people to adapt to an alien set of values—including a core belief that they are inferior. This results in deep psychological trauma.

Fanon's work played a pivotal role in the civil rights movements of the 1960s.

Macat analyses are available from all good bookshops and libraries.

Access hundreds of analyses through one, multimedia tool.
Join free for one month **library.macat.com**

Macat Pairs

Analyse historical and modern issues from opposite sides of an argument. Pairs include:

INTERNATIONAL RELATIONS IN THE 21ST CENTURY

Samuel P. Huntington's
The Clash of Civilisations

In his highly influential 1996 book, Huntington offers a vision of a post-Cold War world in which conflict takes place not between competing ideologies but between cultures. The worst clash, he argues, will be between the Islamic world and the West: the West's arrogance and belief that its culture is a "gift" to the world will come into conflict with Islam's obstinacy and concern that its culture is under attack from a morally decadent "other."

Clash inspired much debate between different political schools of thought. But its greatest impact came in helping define American foreign policy in the wake of the 2001 terrorist attacks in New York and Washington.

Francis Fukuyama's
The End of History and the Last Man

Published in 1992, *The End of History and the Last Man* argues that capitalist democracy is the final destination for all societies. Fukuyama believed democracy triumphed during the Cold War because it lacks the "fundamental contradictions" inherent in communism and satisfies our yearning for freedom and equality. Democracy therefore marks the endpoint in the evolution of ideology, and so the "end of history." There will still be "events," but no fundamental change in ideology.

Macat Pairs

Analyse historical and modern issues from opposite sides of an argument. Pairs include:

HOW TO RUN AN ECONOMY

John Maynard Keynes's
The General Theory OF Employment, Interest and Money

Classical economics suggests that market economies are self-correcting in times of recession or depression, and tend toward full employment and output. But English economist John Maynard Keynes disagrees.

In his ground-breaking 1936 study *The General Theory*, Keynes argues that traditional economics has misunderstood the causes of unemployment. Employment is not determined by the price of labor; it is directly linked to demand. Keynes believes market economies are by nature unstable, and so require government intervention. Spurred on by the social catastrophe of the Great Depression of the 1930s, he sets out to revolutionize the way the world thinks

Milton Friedman's
The Role of Monetary Policy

Friedman's 1968 paper changed the course of economic theory. In just 17 pages, he demolished existing theory and outlined an effective alternate monetary policy designed to secure 'high employment, stable prices and rapid growth.'

Friedman demonstrated that monetary policy plays a vital role in broader economic stability and argued that economists got their monetary policy wrong in the 1950s and 1960s by misunderstanding the relationship between inflation and unemployment. Previous generations of economists had believed that governments could permanently decrease unemployment by permitting inflation—and vice versa. Friedman's most original contribution was to show that this supposed trade-off is an illusion that only works in the short term.

Macat analyses are available from all good bookshops and libraries.

Access hundreds of analyses through one, multimedia tool.
Join free for one month **library.macat.com**

Printed in the United States
by Baker & Taylor Publisher Services